CW01068601

DO YOUR OWN HOME SECURITY

Defend Your Property and Reduce Your Insurance

Jack Hay & Ian Penberthy

W. Foulsham & Co. Ltd.
London · New York ·
Toronto · Cape Town · Sydney

W. Foulsham & Company Limited
Yeovil Road, Slough, Berkshire, SL1 4JH

ISBN 0–572–01329–9

Printed in Great Britain at the Bath Press, Bath

CONTENTS

	Introduction	4
1.	How Vulnerable is Your Home?	5
2.	Simple Precautions	8
3.	Locks	11
4.	Marking Property	24
5.	Lock Up or Hide?	31
6.	Security Lighting	41
7.	Identifying Callers	49
8.	Alarms	56
9.	Insurance	78
10.	Safety in the Home	82
	Information Sources	95
	Index	96

INTRODUCTION

The fact that you are reading this book shows that you are concerned, if only in a small way, about protecting your home, your possessions and your family from the worst effects of the steady rise in crime against the individual. You may know someone who has suffered at the hands of the criminal element in our society, you may have first-hand experience yourself, or you may simply be worried about the all-too-familiar newspaper stories of criminal activity; it doesn't matter why you are taking an interest in protecting you and yours, it's just important that you do something about it.

The purpose of this book is twofold: to make you aware of the risks you face from criminals - not just the professionals but also the opportunists whom you may tempt unwittingly – and to show you just what you can do to outwit these villains. It comes at a time when there is increasing demand from the public for simple, yet effective, security systems and equipment that are reasonably priced and designed specifically for the domestic market. This demand is being met by many manufacturers who, given the immense popularity of DIY activities, have developed quite sophisticated systems that can be installed by the average practical person with a considerable saving in cost compared to professionally installed systems.

This book will show you all the options and help you decide on the best course of action. Knowing that you have considered all the possibilities and chosen the best will give you considerable peace of mind in addition to the obvious sense of security you will gain from knowing the physical measures you have taken. Never become complacent, however; remember, the criminal is only waiting for you to drop your guard. Never give him the upper hand.

1
HOW VULNERABLE IS YOUR HOME?

It's surprising just how easy it is for a burglar to break into a house; carelessness, neglect or a lack of maintenance on the part of the householder will often allow the villain to walk right in. Once in, he will establish an escape route and then set about helping himself to your most valued possessions; he may amuse himself still further by wrecking the place as well. All homes are vulnerable to burglary but some parts are more vulnerable than others, so if you have done nothing about increasing home security before, now is the time to make a thorough inspection of your defences. Note the weak points and then, using the information in the rest of this book, do something about improving the situation.

When you make your inspection, put yourself in a burglar's shoes; stand back and ask yourself where would be the easiest place to break in. In the past you may have been unlucky enough to have locked yourself out. How did you get back in? Was it easy? You may have been able to reach a window that you always leave open for ventilation using the handy ladder you keep in the unlocked garden shed, or perhaps you had to break a small pane of glass to reach a door or window handle, or even had to dig out the putty and remove a complete pane intact? Obviously, in such a situation, you would be very careful to cause the least amount of damage, but a burglar would have no qualms about doing a considerable amount of damage in an attempt to break in. Systematically look at each outer door and window, checking for weakness in structure or fittings and ease of access.

CHECKING WINDOWS

The windows are probably the most vulnerable part of your home; they have easily-broken, large panes of glass and often thin breakable wooden frames. Ground floor windows will be the most accessible so inspect these first.

Thieves don't like to be seen at work so one of the first things you should look for are windows that are partially or totally concealed from the view of neighbours or passers-by – by fences, walls, hedges, bushes, trees, etc. Rotten wooden frames can easily be wrenched from the window opening and loose frames that rattle in the wind indicate that there is a gap large enough to insert a jemmy to lever them open or to slide a thin blade in to flip a catch open. Sometimes a badly fitting transom window can be jarred sufficiently to spring the stay free of its rest. Broken window panes also offer the burglar a good starting point. While you are thinking about the windows, have you or any previous owner done anything about fitting window locks? The normal arrangement of a stay and catch is fine for holding the window closed to keep out the weather but it certainly won't keep out the burglar.

Don't be lulled into thinking that if your ground floor windows are well protected, you need not worry about those on upper floors. Thieves often come in through upstairs windows – many conveniently left open for ventilation – and there are usually plenty of means available to them for scaling the walls. Drainpipes and soil pipes often run close to bathroom windows and are easily climbed. A ground-floor extension (particularly if flat roofed) provides a handy stepping stone as does an adjoining garage. Tall, mature trees can be as good as having a ladder, but then of course the householder often provides the ladder himself – a surprising number are left in unprotected outbuildings or even hung on an outside wall.

Even roof windows are at risk from burglars, particularly if the intruder has done a bit of roofing work and has no fear of heights or of clambering about on a steeply sloping roof.

INSPECT THE OUTER DOORS

Next, turn your attention to both the front and back doors – and any others such as patio doors or french windows. Once again, could anyone work on them concealed by, say, a solid sided porch? The front door may be hidden by a garage or by a large shrub or a tree in the garden. If the frame is loose or rotten, it can soon be levered out and if there is a large gap between the door and frame the two could be levered apart, or a simple spring latch forced open with a plastic card. Doors with glass panels are particularly bad; once the glass is broken it is a simple matter to reach in to operate the catch and/or bolts. What about the locks? Are they strong security locks or are they easily-forced cheap latches? Are there door chains or limiters on each door? And a viewer so you can see who is calling?

Remember to include any outbuildings in your inspection since they often contain valuable items and may provide a good selection of house-breaking tools which the burglar can put to good use. Keeping a burglar out of these is just as important as keeping him out of the house so strong locks and sound window and door frames are essential. In extreme cases, an integral garage can provide a concealed area where a burglar can smash through the wall into the house.

SEEKING PROFESSIONAL ADVICE

Of course you may feel uncertain about just how secure your house is or you may know it has weaknesses but be unsure about the best type of protection to opt for. In either case help is at hand in the shape of the Crime Prevention Officer from your local police station. The job of the Crime Prevention Officer (CPO) is to advise the public on the steps they can take to reduce the risk of them suffering at the hands of criminals. He is specially trained for the job and will come to your home and inspect it from top to bottom. He will point out its weak points and tell you about the sort of security equipment you should install to make it a tough nut for the burglar to crack. You will benefit tremendously from a visit by your local CPO and what's more the service is free.

2
SIMPLE PRECAUTIONS

That old adage about charity beginning at home could equally well be applied to security; the first step in keeping the burglar away is to adopt the right security-conscious attitude. Spending a fortune of sophisticated security products is all very well but if you regularly provide an open invitation to the burglar – and many people do just that – it is money down the drain. Developing the right habits will make life difficult for the thief, and being aware of the invitations you can offer the thief every time you leave your house – even for a short while – will help you keep what is rightfully yours.

UNDER LOCK AND KEY

Protecting your possessions means locking up your house *every* time you leave it unattended. That means shutting and locking all the doors and windows, even the upstairs windows when you go out – every time you go out, even if it is only for a few minutes to go to the post box or a local shop. A few minutes is all the thief needs in many cases. If you leave a small window, such as a transom, open for fresh air or for the cat to come and go, you are asking for trouble; some thieves even have junior assistants who can crawl through very small openings and let their adult accomplice in. If you leave the back door unlocked, you deserve to lose everything; thieves like to use back entrances when breaking into a house since there is less likelihood of them being noticed.

Never leave a front or back door key under a door mat or nearby flower pot, or tied to a piece of string and hung inside the letter box. You might think a thief would never guess where you had hidden the key, but he will; he knows all the likely places to look. Make sure that everyone who needs to come and go has his or her own key.

Whilst on the subject of locking things up, make sure that any side entrance gates are always are locked or bolted securely and that you keep any shed or garage locked. These usually contain a fine selection of tools which a burglar can use to help him break in to your house, and never leave a ladder where it is easily reached. It is surprising how often a handy ladder is left for the thief to try his hand at breaking in through one of the upstairs windows.

Lock up your car, too, even if it is parked in your own driveway – a few moments are all the thief needs to steal something from your car, or the car itself.

MAKING THE HOUSE LOOK OCCUPIED

Thieves don't like the thought of coming face to face with the occupiers of the house they are breaking into, so they will do all they can to make sure that no one is in before they make a start. Sometimes, their life is made easy for them; so many people obligingly leave notes to tell expected callers that they've gone out and will be back in 10, 15, 20 minutes. Just the sort of thing a thief wants to know! Never do this – wait for your caller to arrive. At night, make the house look occupied when you are out by leaving on at least one light and preferably a couple to show at both the front and back (see page 41).

Holiday time is when thieves really have an easy time of things; there are so many indications that clutter up the doorstep or overflow from the letterbox to show that there is no one at home. Whenever you go on holiday make sure you cancel milk and newspaper deliveries, making a point of speaking directly to the milkman and newsagent so that you know they have amended their order books. Milk bottles left on a doorstep for days or a steadily growing wad of newspapers stuffed into the letterbox are sure signs that the house is empty.

Postal deliveries can build up, too, although they can be held until your return on payment of a fee to the post office. You can't control the delivery of free newspapers, however, or you may have a parcel delivered and simply left on the doorstep. The conscientious delivery drivers of the past who would ask a neighbour to take in a parcel seem to be few and far between now. It is common these days for householders to be asked to leave their dustbins out on the pavement when refuse collection is due; if you leave yours out for collection while you are away it will remain outside the house as a sure sign that you are away.

The best solution to these problems is to enlist the aid of a nearby relative or a trusted neighbour who is prepared to make your house look as though it is still occupied by collecting postal deliveries, parcels, newspapers, etc. Someone who will turn on a light each evening and switch it off again in the morning and who will keep an eye on the place for any suspicious goings on. Obviously such a person must be trusted since you should leave a key to the house with them, but you may feel it is asking a lot. Remember, however, that you should offer to do the same for them when they are away.

You should also tell the police that the house will be unoccupied and that you have left the key with a neighbour and who that neighbour is. They won't be able to put a 24 hour watch on the house, but they will keep an eye open for anything suspicious. If you should be unfortunate to have a burglar break in, the police will also make sure that any broken door or window is boarded up until your return.

NEIGHBOURHOOD WATCH SCHEMES

Neighbourhood watch is an American idea which has been enthusiastically received in Britain by many police forces. Wherever the scheme has been introduced there has been a marked decline in crime – burglaries, muggings, vandalism, car theft, etc. The idea is for the public to protect their neighbourhood by reporting anything suspicious they see or hear – either directly to the police or to their local neighbourhood watch co-ordinator. Areas where this type of scheme is in operation are usually clearly signposted so that the thief knows he is going into an area where the inhabitants are on the look out for strangers and unusual goings on.

3
LOCKS

Considered by many to be their first line of defence against the thief, locks are probably the most basic form of security you can buy, and there are plenty of different types to choose from – for both doors and windows. However, choosing the right one for the job is not particularly difficult once you have identified your own particular needs.

One point to bear in mind, though, when you are considering installing new locks is whether the doors, windows and their frames are in sound condition. There is little point in forking out a lot of money on high security locking devices if the doors and windows themselves are weak, or their frames are rotten or loose in their openings. It is not unknown for a thief to lever a window and frame completely from its opening, so check all round the house first and have any defects put right before you fit any extra protection. Invest in hardwood frames – or metal ones – and make sure all external doors are at least $1\frac{1}{2}$ in thick. Repair or replace any damaged or rotten sections. Make sure the windows and doors fit well, too; a warped frame or one where there is a large gap between the window or door and the frame will often allow a thief to insert a pry-bar to lever it open.

LOCKS FOR DOORS

When most people consider improving the security of their home, the first area they will do anything about is the front door. Often, though, the back door is just as much at risk, if not more so; most back doors are of inferior construction when compared to the front and very often they are in a much more secluded position, allowing the thief to work under cover whilst breaking in. So rule number one when considering adding extra locks is to treat both front and back doors in the same way.

Most front doors are fitted with cylinder latches, often called night latches or rim latches, which have a spring-loaded bolt operated by a knob on the inside and by a key from the outside. One face of the bolt is curved so that when the door is pushed or pulled closed it slides over the edge of the staple and then springs out again to lock the door. A sliding catch allows you to lock the bolt in the extended or retracted position. Although very convenient to use, this type of latch is not very secure. Firstly, the latch body and staple are surface mounted to the inner face of the door and frame, and their security relies on the strength of the fixing screws. On a glazed door, all the thief has to do is break the glass, reach in and turn the knob to open the door. If the door is solid, he can always slide a piece of thin, flexible plastic (like a credit card) between door and frame to force back the bolt. If your front door is fitted with this sort of latch, you would be wise to back it up with a second security lock or replace it with something more substantial.

Various replacements are available for the simple night latch and they are usually easy to fit since they occupy the same space. The spring-loaded bolt is the vulnerable part, so any replacement should have a deadlock bolt – that is a bolt that can only be retracted and extended with a key. Most of these locks also have a key-lockable inner knob as well, which can either be set from inside or out. Deadlock bolts are squared off, not curved like those of the night latch, so

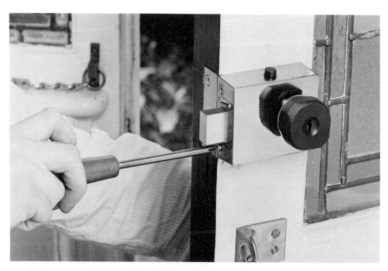

Most front door latches are a security risk. Use a lock that can't be opened by hand through a broken window. Simply install in place of old type.

they cannot be sprung back by a piece of plastic. Make sure that any lock of this type that you buy has a hardened steel bolt and casing so that they cannot be cut or drilled through by the more determined burglar.

Like the night latch, these security replacements have a sliding catch so that the bolt can be held in the retracted position for those occasions when you are in and out a lot (when gardening, for instance). They are best used with a spring-loaded latch of some sort. Some cylinder latches combine a spring-loaded bolt with a key operated deadlock, and a recent innovation includes a latch with 50,000 key combinatios, making it unlikely that a thief would have a duplicate key.

No matter how robust, all cylinder latches have a basic weakness and that is they are surface mounted to the door; by far the strongest locks to fit are those which are housed inside the door and frame – assuming there is adequate material to accommodate them without actually weakening the door. These are known as mortice locks, the best complying with British Standard 3621, which specifies that they must have a five-lever movement and at least 1,000 key permutations.

In a five-lever lock movement there are five pivotting levers with cut-outs that correspond to the shape of the key blade. When the key and lever cut-outs match, the lock can be operated, but if only one of the cut-outs does not match the key, the lock cannot be opened. Such locks are considered safe from lock picks and skeleton keys. Obviously, locks with fewer levers are less secure and really should not be considered for external doors.

Many mortice locks have a deadlock bolt only, but there are versions which incorporate a spring-loaded bolt as well, often operated by a handle or knob on each side of the door, making them ideal for fitting to doors you are in and out of a lot – a back door, for example. Make sure any mortice lock you buy is protected by a hardened steel casing and has a hardened steel bolt.

One of the strong points of the mortice lock is that the burglar must destroy the area of the door and frame around it to break in – unless he can attack the door at another, more vulnerable point. Obviously, the greatest strength is provided in the vicinity of the lock itself, but elsewhere the door might be more vulnerable. With this in mind, recent developments are the multi-point and multi-plane locks. The former fits into the leading edge of the door as a normal lock but it shoots several bolts sideways into the frame at regularly spaced intervals in addition to shooting a bolt into the head of the frame and another into the sill. The multi-plane lock is more ambitious, shooting bolts which run through the centre of the door into the frame at both sides, the head and sill when the key is turned. Obviously, this requires quite a complicated mechanism inside the door and it is not compatible with all types of door. However, complete replacement doors are available with this high-security form of locking.

One of the inevitable consequences of the mass production of locks is duplication of keys, and there is always the worry that a burglar might be able to obtain sufficient keys to crack the more common types of lock. With this in mind, lock manufacturers are concentrating more and more on methods of improving key security. Key shapes can now be registered with manufacturers who will only issue a replacement on receipt of an authorised signature, and one company has introduced a unique double-bladed key with a system of locks to match. This key offers 4,000 million key shape variations with a registration system that means that each key variation is unique to its owner – no one else can get a copy. Another advantage of this particular system is that it covers a very wide range of lock types (even padlocks) so that all domestic applications are provided for. This means that you need only have one key to operate all the locks in the house.

Another type of mortice lock has a push-button keyboard instead of a key; the lock can only be operated by tapping in the owner's personal entry code, but just like having a bank cash card, it requires a good memory, since it would be unwise to write the number down anywhere in case it fell into the wrong hands. These days, it is possible even to buy security locks that incorporate micro-switches for linking to a burglar alarm system; not only do they prevent easy entry by the burglar but they also set off the alarm to scare him away.

BUYING LOCKS

Choosing a strong lock is one thing, but you must also make sure it will fit your door. So when you go to buy take a note with you of the door thickness ($1\frac{1}{2}$ in is the minimum for a mortice lock, and even then it should be a special 'slim' model) and also the width of the door stile (the vertical portion of the door into which the lock fits); you may find that it is too narrow to accept some lock bodies.

Another thing to bear in mind when buying any lock is your ability to fit it. Surface-mounted types are usually no problem and may only need some careful paring with a chisel on the edge of the door to accept the lock body. Often they will fit into the recess already cut for the original night latch. A mortice lock on the other hand requires a deep, narrow recess to be cut into the edge of the door and into the frame, and considerably more skill and care is needed. The amount of material removed (by boring a series of holes with a wood bit and then cleaning out the waste with a bevel-edge chisel) should be the absolute minimum to accept the lock body; if you remove too much you stand the very real chance of weakening the door to the extent that it could be broken open, leaving the lock in place! If you really want the kind of security that mortice locks give, but do not think you can cope with the work involved, call on a locksmith or experienced carpenter to do the job for you, otherwise you will be simply wasting time and money.

ADDITIONAL DOOR SECURITY

Good strong locks go a long way to securing a door, but they should not be relied upon on their own since other areas of the door perimeter may be very vulnerable and allow the insertion of a stout bar so that the complete door can be forcibly levered out.

Heavy-gauge, surface-mounted bolts fitted to the top and bottom of the door so that they shoot up into the head of the door frame and down into the sill or floor will help, but they must be fitted with long (at least $1\frac{1}{2}$ in) screws. On a glazed door, however, they are very vulnerable and a much better idea is to fit rack bolts. These are let into the edge of the door much like a mortice lock and are operated by a special

Don't forget the hinge side of the door either – essential on outward-opening doors. These hinge bolts will prevent forcing or lifting.

splined key through a small keyhole drilled on the inside of the door.

Back doors often open outwards, making their hinges very vulnerable – all the burglar has to do is drive out the hinge pins and lift the door away. The solution is to fit hinge bolts – hardened metal studs set into the back edge of the door next to the hinges. They fit into holes drilled in the door frame when the door is shut, and when teamed with rack bolts provide a very secure method of holding the door in place. It is a good idea to fit hinge bolts to inward opening doors as well as a reinforcement for the hinges.

Door protection should be completed by fitting a good stout door chain or solid bar (known as a door limiter), both of which prevent the door from being opened more than a fraction. This allows you to identify a caller but denies access. Whether you are buying a chain or door limiter, make sure it is of heavy-gauge, hardened steel and that you fit it with strong screws at least $1\frac{1}{2}$ in long. The chain or limiter should be fitted so that the door cannot be opened far enough for a burglar to get his shoulder between the door and frame when open. Some chains fit into a snap lock on the door frame so that you can fit them when you go out, using a key through the narrow gap to release them on your return. One example has a chain similar in appearance to a bicycle chain which retracts into the door when not in use.

LOCKS FOR WINDOWS

Often householders give a lot of thought to securing doors but do nothing about the windows of their homes, yet the windows are more vulnerable than the doors; their frames are weaker, there are large areas of easily broken glass, and they provide large openings for climbing through. Fortunately, there are many locks available for protecting windows, and choosing the right one begins with finding out which type of windows you have: wooden or metal framed; hinged, tilting or sliding. Then look at each window and decide how often you use it. Window locks vary considerably in ease of use; some lock automatically each time you close the window, others must be locked by pushing a button or turning a knob or key, and some have to be screwed shut with a special key. The more complicated or time-consuming the job of locking, the less likely you are to secure the lock each time you go out – which defeats the object of fitting them in the first place. You may find the automatic types to be more expensive, so you can compromise by fitting these to the windows you open most and fit cheaper key-operated or screw-down types to those opened only occasionally.

Wooden-framed windows offer the most possibilities for fitting locks because wood is easy to drill and cut for lock rebates, etc. The strongest locks you can fit to hinged and tilting wooden-framed windows are smaller versions of door rack bolts. Being set into the frame, they are extremely strong and cannot be tampered with.

However, window frames might not always be thick enough to accommodate a rack bolt and so some form of surface-mounted lock must be installed instead. Easiest to use is the type that has a waisted stud on the opening frame and a snap lock on the fixed frame. You simply close the window and it locks automatically, but it must be opened with a special key. Then there are various types that shoot a bolt into a rebate cut in the fixed portion of the frame, either by pushing a button or turning a small knob. All require a key to open them.

Screw-down types include one which has a hasp and staple which are locked together with a threaded stud. Most, however, have a stud which is screwed into a hole in the fixed frame or into a threaded receiver tube set in the frame.

Window bolts, although more difficult to fit, have the benefits of neat appearance and good strength. Also they are very cost-effective.

*Metal window latches can be locked too. Here you can see a 'push-close'
method. No key required for locking but you need key for opening.*

19

Some window locks are screwed into position and are for windows that stay closed. If window is used a lot then go for a push-button type.

They are time-consuming to use, but they do have the advantage of pulling the opening and fixed frames together tightly, preventing a gap which a burglar might use to insert a pry-bar. They help reduce draughts, too.

Sliding wooden sash windows present their own particular locking problems, and the most common way of dealing with them is to fit a device that will stop one sash sliding past the other. Screw-down types similar to those for hinged windows work well here, passing through one sash and into the other. There is also a type of rack bolt which fits into the upper sash and is extended by means of a key to prevent lower sash passing it. Other types of simply screw to the surface of the sash frame and either shoot a bolt into a hole bored in the upper sash or into a receiver plate. Some sash window locks offer two locking positions so that the window can also be secured in a partially open position for ventilation.

Metal-framed windows offer fewer possibilities for locks,

many being surface-mounted with self-tapping screws and throwing a bolt across the face of the fixed frame. However, there are types which fit inside the window opening rebate and are operated by a key through a hole drilled in the frame. These cannot be tampered with.

Most companies, however, merely offer devices for securing the window handle or window stay, which are better than nothing (they can be fitted to wooden windows, too). Handle locks usually comprise a sliding bolt which prevents the handle being turned by pushing against its end, although there is a replacement handle available that incorporates a cylinder lock. Stay locks clamp the stay to its rest, either with a sliding bolt or a screw clamp. They are not always the easiest to use and some take up holes in the stay, restricting its usefulness.

Most of the locks used on normal hinged windows are also suitable for fitting to French windows; they should be installed at the top and bottom of the door that closes last and arranged to shoot their bolts up into the head of the frame and down into the sill.

Sliding windows, including large patio doors, usually run on wheels in a track and they are vulnerable to being levered from this track. They can be secured by fitting a simple push-button lock on the inner window or door. This shoots a bolt into a hole drilled in the frame of the outer window or door, preventing its movement in any direction. Some locks clamp directly to the track to prevent movement, but they will not stop the window or door being levered outwards from the track.

BUYING WINDOW LOCKS

It is important that you buy locks that are suited to the window frame material; wooden-framed windows will need different fixing screws to steel-framed windows, steel-framed windows will need different fixings to aluminium-framed windows, so check the packaging carefully since the locks themselves are often of a universal type. Some locks may need rebates cutting in the frame, and these obviously cannot be arranged in metal frames. If you do intend fitting a lock to a wooden frame that needs a rebate cutting, make sure first that the frame itself is thick enough for this to be cut without weakening the frame; ideally, the rebate width should be a third (or less) of the total width of the frame.

Whenever you buy window locks, always buy at least one for every opening window in the house, doubling up on large windows to provide a spread of protection and prevent a lever being forced into a corner furthest from the lock.

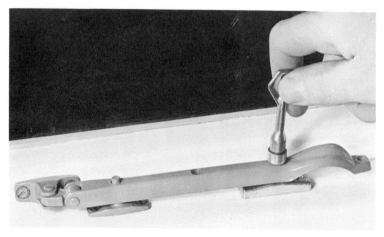

Here's a simple method of retaining this window stay in the locked position. Simple but very effective.

And don't forget the good old fashioned padlock – very versatile in its use. Note the shackle protection offered by the raised shoulders on lock body. Don't go for the cheapest.

Fitting window locks is usually quite simple, provided you can use a drill and screwdriver, and they all come with installation instructions and fixing screws. Surface-mounted locks rely on the strength of their fixings for security, so make sure the screws are substantial and either cover their heads with security plugs (often provided with the lock), fill their slots with car body filler or drill them out to prevent removal.

LOCKS FOR OUTBUILDINGS

Traditionally, garden sheds and garages are protected (if at all) by padlocks and these should be bought with care. Go for quality not cheapness.

Start with a sturdy padbar – that's the hinged flap which secures the door to the lock staple on the door frame. Make sure the bar covers the heads of its own fixing screws and those of the staple when it is closed and the padlock is in place. The better examples are held in place by coach bolts which pass right through the door.

Always choose a heavy-duty padlock, looking for the British Standard 'kite mark' which will give you an indication of its high quality. It should have a hardened-steel shackle which should be as short as possible and thick to prevent cutting with bolt croppers – some padlocks have raised sides that provide additional protection to the shackle once locked, and one type of high-security padlock covers the shackle completely, preventing interference.

4
MARKING PROPERTY

Millions of pounds worth of property is stolen in burglaries every year and though much of it is never recovered, hundreds of thousands of pounds worth of stolen goods does fall into the hands of the police. But catching the culprits and recovering the property is not the end of the matter – many of the items recovered are never returned to their rightful owners, for the simple reason that they cannot be identified.

The obvious way of ensuring positive identification of your property is by marking it clearly. Not only will this help the police return it to you should it be stolen, but the fact that something does carry a mark can be a very strong deterrent to the villain since it will make his life particularly difficult when it comes to disposing of the goods. In fact, one of the first things the police do when they come across any stolen or lost property is check it for identifying marks; they even use ultra-violet lights which will show up the 'invisible' markings made by special security marker pens.

There are many different methods for marking property, but first you must decide just what you are going to mark on it. Whatever it is, you must make sure it is the same for all your belongings, otherwise it could get very confusing. You could just use your initials, or your name perhaps, but to give the police the best chance of returning any stolen property to you, it is best to use your postcode. This pinpoints your town and street and, with the addition of the house number (or first two letters of its name) will provide a positive location from which the item was taken. For example, someone living at 24 Hope Road, Anytown, AN3 4BA, would use the marking: AN3 4BA 24; and someone from Rose Cottage, High Street, Notown, NT9 2LM, would use: NT9 2LM RO. This is by far the best form of identifying mark since there can be no argument as to the place of origin.

The post code is now recommended as a useful identification code to mark on valuables.

Remember to mark all your valuables and anything portable which you might lose.

You should mark this code on everything and anything of value – even sentimental value – which often cannot be replaced despite compensation offered by insurance policies. You should also mark anything portable that you might lose: handbags, cameras, radios and the like.

METHODS OF MARKING

The exact method of marking property will depend on the type of material it is made from; there is a variety of systems available: etching, die stamping, branding, identification paint, indelible marker pens and pens which use an invisible ink. All are quick and easy to use, and inexpensive.

Etching your personal code on to property is probably the most practical of all the marking methods since it can be seen quite clearly and cannot be removed without giving some clue to a potential purchaser that the item in question has been stolen. It will tell the thief that he is going to have problems in disposing of the loot, and problems are just what he does not want.

There are two methods of etching, which is ideal for marking items such as cameras, radios, hi-fi equipment, video recorders, etc, in fact anything with a hard, rigid surface. The first requires the use of a special hard-tipped engraving pen which you can buy complete with a set of letter and number stencils. You simply hold the stencil in place and scratch the shape of the individual letters or numbers on to the surface with the tip of the pen.

The second method of etching is by acid and, again, kits are available complete with dry-transfer stencil letters and numbers. The stencil transfers are used to mask off the code and the acid is brushed on to etch the area around them. Of the two methods, the first is easier to do and takes but a few minutes.

Etching is a good way of providing extra protection for your car as well – instead of your postcode, etch the registration number into the corner of each window. If a thief takes the car to change its identity for resale, he must change all the glass – an expensive, time-consuming job in which he runs the risk of alerting the glass supplier to what is going on. This method of marking has proved a real deterrent to professional car thieves; if you are not sure about doing it

Etching, using a special hard-tipped engraving pen and a stencil.

Engraving kits are readily available and easy to use to safeguard property.

yourself, there are companies which offer a mobile marking service and will come to your home to do it for you for a modest fee.

Of course, not all materials lend themselves to etching, and you may not want to put such an obvious form of marking on a more valuable or delicate item, particularly if it would be damaged in the process – porcelain or ceramics for instance. For this situation, you can choose to use a security marker pen instead. There are two types: one leaves a clearly visible indelible marking and the other has an invisible ink which can only be read under ultra-violet light. These can be used to mark all manner of materials including clothing, but in the latter case it would be wise to remark them after washing or dry cleaning just to be on the safe side.

With indelible marker pens, it is best to put the marking on a concealed surface, since there is less likelihood of the thief removing or defacing it. For china and ceramics there is a special pen available which uses a metallic compound to mark the item without breaking through the glaze.

Die stamping is ideal for large metal items such as tools and bicycles, and most police crime prevention units are

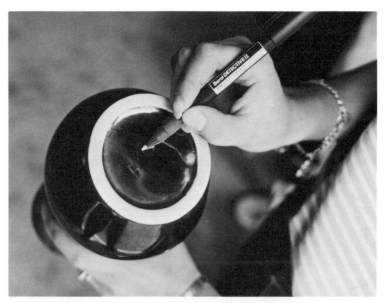

Many indelible markers use an ink which is only visible under ultra-violet light.

Die stamping is ideal for large metal items.

prepared to stamp your postcode on to the frame of your bicycle using a set of special punches (some bicycles shops will do it too). This is probably the most effective way of identifying stolen bicycles and it has been proved to protect against bicycle thieves who have been known to leave marked cycles in favour of examples they can get rid of easily.

If you don't know your postcode, ask at your local post office; they will tell you what it is. But some people may not want to use the postcode system, for the simple reason that they travel around a lot. In this situation, you can subscribe to a computerised marking system. Each subscriber is allocated a personal code number which is stored together with the subscriber's name and address (easily changed at any time) in the computer's memory. The company then supplies an electric engraving tool, stencil and marker pen so that the code can be marked on all items of value. The police have 24-hour access to the information in the computer and need only quote the code number over the telephone to be given the subscriber's name and address.

Of course marking your property might well deter the burglar from taking it, but that doesn't stop him breaking in or attempting to if he thinks there are easy pickings to be had. For this reason, most security marking kits provide adhesive labels for sticking into house or car windows to warn would-be thieves that the property is marked. This may well be enough to send them on their way.

KEEPING RECORDS

You may find that some of the items you own are not suitable for marking or you may not want to mark them, particularly if they are rare and valuable or if the marking will mar the item. In such cases, it is a wise move to keep a record of any details that will help identification. Keep a note of any serial numbers you find each time you buy something new, jotting them down in your diary or telephone book. Some things you own might not have any serial numbers, of course, particularly delicate items like jewellery or antiques. The most effective way of keeping a record of these is to photograph them, preferably in colour. When you take the photograph pay particular attention to any unusual features (hallmarks, crests, initials, etc). To aid identification further, give some scale to the object by placing it next to a rule when you take the photograph, or alongside something else of known size (coins, for example).

Keep a note of the marks you put on your property together with other details and any photographs in a safe place, and for added security ask a friend or relative to keep a copy of the information and the negatives of the photographs. That way, if some disaster befalls your own records you will always be able to duplicate the information.

Whichever method you use to identify your property, you will be striking another blow against crime and you'll be sure that if anything ever does go missing there's a very good chance that you'll get it back.

5
LOCK UP OR
HIDE?

All of us have something we couldn't bear to lose – it might be some jewellery, something of sentimental value, some important documents, perhaps, or even quantities of cash which we like to have at hand. We can do a lot to keep the thief away from those valuable possessions by spending a lot of effort and money on securing the outer defences of our homes with locks and alarm systems, but what if the thief does manage to get in? What else can be done to protect our most valuable property?

The simplest way you can make life difficult for the thief is to hide away any items of value in unlikely places, places you wouldn't expect to find them in. Have a look around your home for unlikely hiding places: airing cupboards, broom cupboards, even under the floor if you can remove a section of floorboard (make sure it isn't left loose, though, in case a tell-tale squeak leads the thief right to it – secure it with magnetic cupboard door catches.). There are probably many other places you can think of – they won't provide total protection, but they will slow up the thief and he doesn't like that.

Of course you could consider installing a safe. Many may scoff at the idea, believing it to be an extreme and expensive solution to the problem, but neither is the case. In fact the steady rise in burglaries and constantly rising insurance premiums have boosted sales in domestic safes and encouraged safe manufacturers to offer a wide range of products to choose from, ranging from disguised cash boxes to free-standing safes of considerable size. Many insurance companies may even insist you have a safe if you have something of particular value and may refuse to insure it if you don't buy a safe; others may offer a reduction in premiums if you keep valuable items in a safe. In this situation, the insurance company should be able to provide you with a list of manufacturers whose products meet with their approval, and it is always worth checking with your insurers to make sure any safe you do buy is approved by them, otherwise you many not get the premium reduction you were hoping for. Some people are even buying safes in preference to insuring their valuables, preferring the one-off payment to regular, increasing premiums.

If you do decide to buy a safe, it is important that you get one that will meet your needs, not just now but in the future when you may have more property to lock away. Many domestic safes are quite small and will only hold limited amounts of jewellery, cash or documents – not much good if you want to lock up the family silver. The checklist on page 40 will help in deciding what to go for.

SMALL SAFES AND CASH BOXES

Of course, the items you wish to keep locked away might have little monetary value and might not be worth the expense of a proper safe. In this case, you might be better off with one of the smaller versions or perhaps a disguised cash box. Although not as strong as a more conventional safe, their small size allows them to be hidden in unlikely places quite easily and this is their main defence.

One very small safe comprises a narrow metal tube which is hammered into a hole drilled in a wall or floor and which provides a housing for a locking cartridge about 2 in diameter. The cartridge is just big enough to hold small amounts of cash or jewellery. Because of its small size it is very easily concealed but would only be suitable for holding perhaps one or two items of jewellery or rolls of banknotes.

Other types of small safe are in the form of strong metal boxes which can be bolted to the floor or the bottom of a wardrobe; they are best when fitted somewhere where they can be covered up by other items, and will provide protection against the casual thief or vandal. Such safes are ideal for fitting in the boot of your car or in a caravan to hold valuable items when you are on holiday.

Strength may not be a major selling point of these small

Not so much a safe – more of a hiding place! This cartridge fits into the wall and will hold valuable small items.

safes but in recent years they have become increasingly sophisticated, and some versions even incorporate alarms and smoke cartridges that go off when the safe is tampered with.

WALL SAFES

Mention the word safe to most people and there is a very good chance they will think of a wall safe; we see them so often in films and on TV. While they can be very secure, they do have certain important drawbacks.

One of the biggest problems with a wall safe is that of size, and in particular depth. In an older house with solid outer walls the maximum depth of hole you could safely make would be by the removal of one layer of bricks and that would give 4-5 in. Modern houses have cavity walls where the outer walls have a 2 in gap between the inner and outer leaves of the wall, and athough the cavity provides extra depth you may still run into problems with anchoring the safe securely. One company actually makes use of the cavity by incorporating struts which extend from the sides of their safe behind the inner leaf of the wall so that if a thief attempted to break it out of the wall he would have to remove a large area of brickwork to do so. One way extra depth could be obtained would be to fit the safe into a disused chimney breast, although some means of anchoring the back of the safe would still be necessary.

Installation is relatively straightforward. After marking out the area for the hole, the plaster is removed with a bolster chisel and then the brickwork removed. Take care in cavity walls not to let any debris fall into the cavity since this may bridge the gap and allow damp to penetrate the inner leaf. For the same reason the mortar on which the safe is bedded must not be allowed to drop down the gap. Fill all round the edge of the safe with mortar, setting the door flush with the face of the wall unless it has a combination lock, in which case the safe must be inset sufficiently for the operating knob to be flush with the wall. (Most safes now come

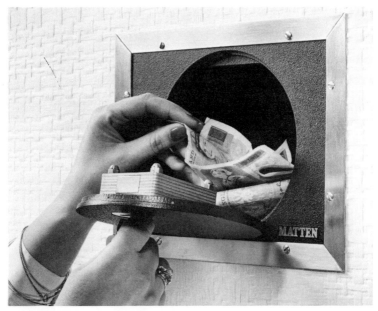

Domestic wall safes can easily be installed. It is important that a site isn't obvious.

with key-operated locks – seven or eight lever locks being common – but combination locks are available on some models).

Site is selected and carefully marked out. Then brick chisel is used to cut bricks.

Once first brick is moved, rest follow relatively easily. Then safe is laid on concrete bed.

It is important that safe stays vertical to the wall and so take care here to hold in position.

When concrete is set the wall face is made good with plaster, ready for decorating.

It is important that a wall safe be cemented into a masonry wall for security; you could bolt one to the timber framework of a plasterboard-faced internal partition wall, but this would offer little resistance to the determined thief. It would be a simple matter to break away the surrounding plaster-board and cut through the framework with a saw to lift out the entire safe and carry it away.

Although the lack of depth can be a problem with a wall safe, it does have the advantage of being easily disguised behind a few books, or in the classic situation behind a picture.

FLOOR SAFES

Floor safes can be installed in both suspended timber floors and solid concrete ones, and in the latter case may qualify for a reduction in premiums from your insurers. It must be said, though, that the installation of a safe in a solid concrete floor can be a very messy business, and if you employ a security firm to do the job the installation costs could double the initial cost of the safe.

Safes designed for fitting to suspended timber floors are made to a size that will fit between a pair of adjacent joists and are secured by bolts passing through the joists. This would be quite a simple job for the average handyman. You would have to choose a position that was accessible (near the edge of the floor or in a corner) and then cut through three or four floorboards so that you could lever them up to expose the joists. The joist positions will be clearly indicated by the rows of nails holding the boards down, and you need to cut the boards flush with the edges of the joists on either side of the pair to which the safe will be bolted. Cut them with a padsaw and when you come to refit them screw battens to the sides of the joists and screw the boards to these. You must take care, though, not to cut through any cables or water pipes for obvious reasons. Once you have bolted the safe in place, you can trim the boards to fit round its opening.

However, the bolted installation is not totally secure – although it may be your only solution, particularly if you live in a flat that is not on the ground floor. A much better idea would be to float a concrete raft between the joists and

Small items of value can be safely protected in an underfloor safe hidden beneath the carpet.

embed the safe in this. The important point to remember when doing this is to set a layer of damp-proof course material between the underside of the joists and the cement, otherwise they may be attacked by damp and will rot.

If you already have a solid concrete floor, the job can be quite involved, but it will result in a very secure installation. Some form of powered excavation equipment will be needed to break through the floor and form a hole large enough for the safe and its surrounding collar of reinforced concrete. Points to watch here are underfloor pipes and heating systems, so take care when planning the safe's position. Also, you will almost certainly break through the floor's damp-proof membrane – usually heavy-gauge polythene sheeting – and this must be made good if you are to avoid problems with rising damp. This is done by lining the hole with more polythene.

Once the safe has been set in place and its top levelled with the floor surface, steel reinforcing rods are fitted round it and the concrete poured in. After levelling concrete, it should be left for a week or 10 days to cure before using the safe.

FREESTANDING SAFES

The major advantage of freestanding safes is that they come in sizes ranging from a couple of feet square right up to bank vault size, so there should be no problem in finding one to accommodate all your valuable possessions – even the bulkiest. Don't assume that size guarantees security, though; some of the smallest safes are often the strongest. As a guide to a safe's strength you can go on the price (the more expensive it is, the stronger it is likely to be) and on the amount of money an insurance company would let you keep in it and still cover you for its loss.

Another advantage of the freestanding safe is that you can take it with you if you move house. Though initially it may be more expensive than a wall or floor safe, this portability can make it a more attractive proposition in the long run. If you choose a freestanding safe, make sure the floor where it will stand is strong enough to support it – no problem with a solid concrete floor, but a suspended timber floor may need reinforcing; check with the supplier.

PROTECTION FROM FIRE

Many safes are described by their manufacturers as being both thief and fire resistant, but this can be misleading. In order to provide protection against a thief, a safe must contain a high proportion of metal, and metal is an excellent conductor of heat. A true fire safe uses very little metal in its construction for obvious reasons; therefore, the two do not lend themselves to amalgamation. However, in the average house fire, the peak of heat is produced over a period of 15–20 minutes and when manufacturers say that a thief-resistant safe is also fire resistant they usually mean that for this short period, the temperature inside will not rise sufficiently to incinerate the contents. Unfortunately, they cannot guarantee this.

Underfloor safes in solid floors stand the best chance of protecting their contents from fire since they are surrounded by concrete and the fire will be above them. But if the main reason for wanting a safe is to protect important documents that are of no value to anyone else, you would be better off buying a proper fire safe.

CHOOSING A SAFE

There are plenty of domestic safes on the market and choosing the right one can be confusing. Use this checklist to make the job easier:

1   Consider carefully what you intend keeping in the safe and make sure you buy one large enough.

2   Make sure the safe you buy has been built to protect risks to the value of its contents.

3   If you are hoping for a reduction in insurance premiums, check with your insurers that the safe you intend buying is acceptable to them.

4   When considering the capital cost of the safe bear in mind the additional cost of installation. Get several quotes.

5   Are you certain you need a security safe? Would a fire safe be better?

6   Do you need a traditional security safe? Would a disguised cash box be better?

7   Decide on a convenient position to install the safe, somewhere where you won't have to dismantle half a wardrobe or rearrange all the room's furniture to get at it.

Choose the safe that most suits your particular needs. Underfloor safe (left); wall safe (right).

6
SECURITY LIGHTING

Because burglars don't want to attract attention to themselves they won't want to be seen lurking around your house. They may try to break in quickly through the front door but at night they are more likely to nip round the back where they can work in the shadows unnoticed and undisturbed. So lighting has an important role to play outdoors as well as indoors by illuminating the approaches to your house and ensuring that there are no dark areas in which the burglar can lurk.

Lighting is such a simple subject, but intelligent use of lights indoors plus careful siting of lights outdoors can provide considerable protection for your home and its contents.

MAKING THE MOST OF INDOOR LIGHTING

Even the closest fitting curtains will allow some chink of light to show through a window at night, and if you stand outside your house you will see just how much light does show. So one of the simplest measures you can take to sow a seed of doubt in the burglar's mind is to leave a light or preferably a couple of lights switched on whenever you are away from the house at night – even if this means leaving them on all day as well. These will go unnoticed during the day but at night they will be seen, even from behind drawn curtains. Faced with this situation, the thief will be unsure of what to do. He may even try knocking at the door or telephoning, but if he receives no reply he still can't be positive that there is no one at home.

Try to leave a light showing at both front and rear of the house, just as you might when you are at home – a hallway

41

and kitchen or lounge, perhaps. If you normally retire early it is a good idea to leave a landing and/or hallway light on all night for security. This has the added advantage of being a safety measure if there are old or very young people in the house who are likely to get up during the night.

If you are likely to be out for a long time, you may feel that leaving lights on in the house is a waste of electricity, but at current prices it costs no more than a couple of pence to keep a 60 watt bulb burning for four hours – a small price to pay for the security it will undoubtedly provide.

AUTOMATIC CONTROL FOR INDOOR LIGHTS

However, there are more economical ways of showing lights at night, even if you are away for several days at a time. By using automatic programmable switching devices you can arrange for lights, and in some instances other electrical appliances like TVs and radios, to be turned on and off at preset times every night or at different times each night. Some of these automatic switches can be programmed for up to seven days in advance, whereas others will continue to run through the set on-off programme every night until you change the programme.

Automatic switches come in two basic forms: a plate-switch to replace the normal wall-mounted light switch and a plug-in device which fits between the plug of a portable appliance (table or standard lamp, radio, TV, etc) and its wall socket.

The plateswitch timer is a direct replacement for the standard wall switch, being exactly the same size and fitting a standard mounting box. It can be used for both one-way and two-way switching and when not in use as a timer provides normal on-off switching of the light. Installation is simple: turn off the light circuit power by removing the appropriate fuse from the consumer unit, unscrew the old switch plate, disconnect the wires and reconnect them to the same terminals of the new switch, refit the switchplate, restore the power and check its operation.

Various types of switch are available: with some you programme the time you want the light to come on and the

A timer control can be used for switching on and off lamps, radio, etc.

number of hours it is to burn; others have a random switching facility which will turn the light off at a slightly different time each night, giving a much more realistic impression that someone is home; yet another type incorporates a photocell which turns the light on automatically as daylight fades and then keeps the light burning for a preset period.

The normal plug-in timer has a clock face on which the 'on' and 'off' times are set. Then you plug it into a 13 amp three-pin socket and plug the appliance to be controlled into the timer. One type offers a push-button setting with a digital readout of times plus the facility to programme up to three 'on' and three 'off' settings at once.

An important point to remember with the plug-in fitting when connected to a standard or table lamp is that the lamp unit must be clear of curtains or anything else that could be a fire risk. Remember, you won't be there when that light comes on and the careless placing of a lamp could easily start a fire; then, instead of protecting a few valuable possessions from the burglar, you might end up losing everything, including the roof over your head.

THE ADVANTAGES OF OUTDOOR LIGHTING

Lighting outdoors has advantages beyond that of discouraging the would-be thief: it means that you will no longer have to fumble for a door key in the dark; that visitors won't have to stumble along darkened pathways or trip down unseen steps; and that you will get greater pleasure from your garden by seeing it softly illuminated at night or by being able to hold summer evening barbecues or parties on a lit patio. A light over a door will not only prevent a burglar working his way through the door but will also allow you to see who callers are at night if you have installed a door viewer (see page 49).

Though termed security lighting, the fittings need not be so obviously functional as the term suggests; indeed, there is a very wide range of attractive and decorative outdoor lighting fittings to choose from, many of which will actually enhance the appearance of your house. There are bulkhead fittings which mount flat to the wall, pendant lanterns, lights on brackets for wall mounting, period style carriage lamps, and ceiling-mounted lights for fitting inside porches. For lighting the garden you can choose from reproduction Victorian 'gas' lamps, modern bollard or post mounted fittings or various types of wall-mounted fittings, including flood-lights. Many outdoor lights make use of tungsten halogen bulbs which are long lasting and very bright while others have miniature fluorescent tubes which are economic to use and provide a soft glow. Their diffusers may be of clear or opaque glass or toughened plastic which is ideal if the lights are in a position where they are likely to be at risk of attack by vandals.

SITING OUTDOOR LIGHTS

The object of outdoor security lighting is to banish shadows and dark corners which the burglar can use to approach the house and get to work unseen; you don't need to recreate the 'Blackpool Illuminations' – you'll probably upset your neighbours if you do – but rather carefully site a few fittings in key positions around the house and in the garden to

Outdoor lighting has other uses too. This wall is highlighted to avoid somebody falling over the edge! Low voltage lamps from Superswitch Ltd.

It is recommended that lights should be used throughout the hours of darkness – electricity use is minimal. This lamp from Marlin Lighting.

provide a good overall spread of light.

Start by fitting a light above or to one side of both the front and back doors, then add wall-mounted fittings to illuminate the sides of the house. Lights on brackets at the corners of walls are particularly effective since they will throw light along two walls at once. You can use a garage lead lamp plugged into a socket in the house to work out the position for each lamp so that you get the best spread of light from it. If you have a patio you could fit spotlights at each end to give a fairly high level of light so that it can be used during summer evenings. In the garden arrange light positions so that they cover pathways and steps and any other approach to the house that might be used by a burglar. Also use them to show up attractive features of the garden such as shrubs, rockeries, ponds. etc.

CONTROLLING OUTDOOR LIGHTS

To be effective, outdoor lights should be switched on at dusk and remain on all night for every night of the year, not just when you are about to go out for the night. Nor should you switch them on every evening you are home and then leave them off when you go on holiday – this provides the thief with just the kind of information he needs. If you can't find a trusty neighbour to switch on your lighting every night while you are away it is better to leave the lighting switched on permanently. However, in the latter case this may arouse the suspicions of a thief if he passes your house regularly during the day and you would be much better off controlling the lights with a programmable switch which will turn them off and on at set times each night, as mentioned previously.

An alternative method of automatic control of outdoor lighting is a photocell which will switch the lights on as dusk falls and switch them off again at dawn. This type of control is particularly useful since it can be left to switch the lights on and off every day of the year, relieving you of the chore and making sure that the lights are always turned on at the right time.

In some cases you may want to switch on outdoor lights for a specific purpose – putting the car away, for example, if the light is over the garage door. In this situation it is possible to fit an outdoor switch which incorporates an infra-red remote control device operated by a small handset, much like a TV remote controller. With this you can switch the lights on from as much as 15 m (50 ft) away. Another type of remote control switch unit for outdoor installation makes use of passive infra-red to detect your approach and switch on the light for you. Such a device could be linked to a spotlight aimed at likely approach paths and used to illuminate a would-be intruder with a sudden bright light which would scare him off quickly.

PROVIDING POWER FOR OUTDOOR LIGHTS

Installing outdoor lighting is not difficult, but unless you are confident of handling the wiring side of the job you must get a qualified electrician to do it for you. Remember, electricity can cause serious injury or even death so it is not something to be toyed with. However, provided you are careful there is no reason why you should not do the whole job yourself.

With lights attached to the house you can normally arrange to take power from the downstairs lighting circuit – remember to isolate the circuit by removing its fuse from the consumer unit before you do any work on the wiring.

First you cut into the circuit cable and join a spur cable to it with a 3-terminal junction box; the cable you use must be 1.0 mm^2 PVC sheathed two-core and earth cable which is the standard size for lighting. The spur cable is run to near the lighting position where it is connected to a 4-terminal junction box and from this individual cables run to the light and its switch. With wall-mounted lights try to arrange for the cable to enter the fitting from behind which will make the installation much neater and the cable less vulnerable. Drill the hole for the cable through the wall so that it slopes upwards from the outside to prevent water running in. Also, make sure you fit the exposed earth cores of the cable with green/yellow earth sleeving to insulate them.

It is important that you don't overload the lighting circuit, and the total wattage of all the bulbs connected to it should be no more than 1000 watts. If your additional outdoor lights will bring the loading above this figure, you should lay in a new circuit specifically for the outdoor lights. This should be run from a spare 5-amp fuseway in the consumer unit. Whether running several lamps from the dowstairs lighting circuit or a new circuit, you can arrange for them all to be operated by one switch or for each lamp to have its own individual switch.

With garden lighting, you can run the cable from the consumer unit indoors through plastic conduit buried in the ground – it must be at least 500 mm (20 in) deep and the conduit joints must be glued with a solvent-weld adhesive to seal them. All cable entry holes in the fittings must be sealed with a non-setting mastic. Similarly, if you want to run the cable along a wall, it should be protected in conduit. The cable itself must be connected to the consumer unit through an Earth Leakage Circuit Breaker which will turn off the power instantly if the cable should be accidentally broken.

As a much safer alternative to using mains electricity in the garden, it is possible to buy lighting kits which use a 12 volt supply from a transformer plugged into a socket in the house. The kits usually contain bollard type lights, low voltage wiring and the transformer. The wiring can be buried in the ground or clipped to walls without fear of receiving a dangerous electric shock if you should cut it accidentally while working in the garden.

7
IDENTIFYING CALLERS

It is a wise precaution to always check on the identity of any stranger who comes to your door – day or night – and actually being able to see callers from behind a strong locked door will give you a better opportunity of deciding whether or not to let them in. Never open the door slightly and peer round the edge; this will allow the criminal to get his shoulder behind it, hence the importance of fitting a strong door chain or limiter (see page 17) which should always be in place when you open the door.

There are various ways you can check on a caller before opening the door; they range from a simple spy-hole door viewer to a closed-circuit television (CCTV) system with a telephone link and electrically-operated door lock. Even simpler is to have a glazed panel in the door, but this should not be too large or it will allow the determined burglar to smash it and reach the locks inside, and it may be embarrasing because any caller will see you just as clearly as you can see them. The purpose-made viewing systems allow you to see without being seen.

TYPES OF DOOR VIEWER

There is quite a range of door viewers to choose from; they come in different sizes to match different thicknesses of door and in various finishes (brass and chrome are popular) to complement or contrast with the finish of the door. All are easy to fit, the job being well within the capability of anyone who can use a hand drill.

The most basic door viewer is the spy-hole type which is very small and hardly noticeable once installed. It comprises a special wide-angle lens attached to the end of a brass tube. The lens gives an angle of view between 160° and 190°

depending on the make and type, meaning that in some cases you can literally look round corners! With such a viewer you can see all of the person standing outside, even if they are very close to the door or standing to one side. An eyepiece tube completes the viewer and sometimes this will have a pivotting flap to prevent light escaping at night.

Door viewers are simple to install. This one views at 90 degrees – which means that you can see around corners!

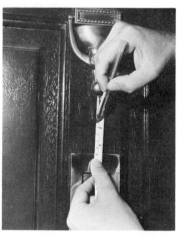

A measure is used to ensure that location is centre to other fittings. Make sure that viewer is at eye level.

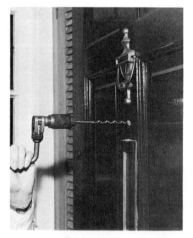

Now a simple matter of drilling hole. Purchase drill bit of correct size to be sure of perfect fit. Also saves time.

Unobtrusive and allows a good view of porch area so that more than one caller can be identified.

Fitting the spy-hole viewer is simplicity itself and can be done in a matter of minutes. Simply use a wood-boring bit to drill a hole through the door to match the diameter of the viewer's body. It is best to drill the hole from the outside of the door, but stop just as the tip of the bit breaks through on the inside. Then finish the hole from the inside; this way, you won't splinter the inner face of the door as the drill breaks through. Insert the lens piece from the outside and the eyepiece from the inside and simply screw the two sections together.

Another larger type of viewer does away with the lens in favour of a two-way mirror; you can look out through the mirrored glass but no one can see in. Another feature of this particular viewer is that the mirror can be pivotted out of the way to leave a small opening through which you can speak to the caller. There is also a hinged metal flap on the inside, allowing you to seal the viewer off.

For a door viewer to be usable both day and night you must fit a light above or to one side of the door and this should be left on all night for additional security (see page 44)

ENTRY PHONES

Although the door viewer is fine for seeing who is at the door in many domestic situations, there are many others where it is not. An elderly or infirm person might have difficulty in reaching a door quickly to see who is calling, particularly if flights of stairs have to be negotiated. Similarly, someone living in a block of flats or divided house with a lockable street door leading to a shared entry-way might find the trek to the door particularly tiresome everytime someone called.

One solution to this problem is the entry phone. This comprises a combined speaker/microphone at the street door linked to a handset inside the house or in each individual flat. The street door is held closed by an electrically–operated latch which is controlled remotely by the occupant. In response to hearing the door bell or buzzer, the occupant can use the handset to determine the reason for the call and use the remote control to open the street door which is usually fitted with a door closer so that it locks automatically.

CLOSED-CIRCUIT TV FOR DOMESTIC USE

Rapid development in the field of electronics plus the increasing popularity of video equipment for home use has meant that CCTV technology in now available for domestic use and at a reasonable price. Of course, there would be little point in installing such a system with the object of maintaining a continuous watch of the approaches to your house since you would not have the time to do it nor the stamina to stay alert for long. However, an important use for CCTV in the home is in seeing who is at the door, and in this respect it is particularly useful for an elderly person or invalid who may have trouble in reaching the door to answer calls. Many systems incorporate a sound as well or can be teamed with an entry phone, and with the addition of a remotely controlled electric door latch would provide the ideal solution to the problem of identifying callers and letting them in, particularly in blocks of flats. A monitor in each flat could be linked with the single outdoor camera.

Of course, as with a door viewer, good lighting is essential around the doorway if the CCTV system is to be usable both day and night. Some cameras incorporate a projector light which comes on when the camera is activated but in most cases a camera should be able to operate satisfactorily on the kind of light levels provided by normal outdoor security lighting. The value of outdoor lighting has already been discussed (see page 44) as has the need for it to be left on all night. With a CCTV system it has the added advantage of preventing the thief from knowing if you are watching or not, whereas with the camera-activated light he will know for sure if you are there or not. A good level of outdoor lighting will also provide protection for the camera itself which may be subjected to vandalism. If a fixed camera is installed the correct lighting level only needs to cover a small area where the caller will stand; however, if a movable camera is used the lighting level must be high over the entire area within range of the camera lens.

CCTV systems for domestic use are available in kit form and should not cost more than a few hundred pounds. A typical kit would comprise a fixed-position camera with microphone and projector light, a camera mounting bracket, a small black and white TV monitor and a length of cable to connect the camera to the monitor. From this you can see that installation is quite straightforward: fix the camera and its bracket to the wall near the door, connect the camera to the monitor indoors with the lead supplied, plug in the monitor, turn it on and adjust the camera position to cover the correct area. Normally the monitor will have several

Here a caller can speak to the occupant. A camera above the door identifies the caller. The door lock can be released by remote control.

channels, one being used to pick up signals from the camera and the others being suitable for picking up normal TV signals.

If the only reason for installing a CCTV system is to provide a check on who is at the door, a fixed position camera is all that is needed. However, this type of equipment is becoming increasingly sophisticated and it is possible to buy remotely operated scanning cameras which will pan from side to side and up and down. Further refinements include a zoom lens for obtaining close-ups (ideal for examining identification documents), a device to allow several cameras to be connected to the monitor at once with selective switching and a facility for recording the camera's picture on a video cassette. In most cases such sophistication would be unnecessary in a domestic installation but they show the range of possibilities with such equipment.

Of course a CCTV camera is vulnerable to attack itself and may be subjected to vandalism, particularly as it is a valuable item and also a means of defence against the criminal. It can be protected however by making sure it is installed out of reach up on the wall or secured in a recess in the wall. Alternatively a steel and wire cage can be built round it.

Closed circuit TV is a very effective way of identifying visitors – a typical kit should not cost more than a few hundred pounds.

CHECKING WHETHER CALLERS ARE GENUINE OR NOT

Anyone who comes to your door on official business (from the gas or electricity boards, the local council, police, etc) will have an identity card or some form of distinctive pass – most should carry a photograph and will be sealed in plastic – but the problem lies in knowing whether the pass you are offered is genuine or not. If you have any doubt at all don't let the caller in until you have found some way of checking his identity. If he *is* genuine he can always come back.

The best way to check is to telephone the organisation he says he represents and ask them to verify the name and serial number on the card. If the person at the door gives you a telephone number to call, look it up yourself in the telephone book; he just may be giving you the number of an accomplice.

If you haven't a telephone it is much more difficult to obtain a positive identification. In this situation it is a good idea to prepare yourself beforehand by asking at the various organisations you deal with to see a sample of their identity cards; that way at least you'll have a good idea if you're being shown the genuine article or a fake. Very often gas and electricity workers will be in some form of uniform and most people of this sort will turn up in a distinctively marked vehicle, so it is worth checking to see if such a vehicle is parked in the road outside. If you are still not happy tell the caller that you are going to telephone his employers while he waits outside – he won't know that you haven't got a telephone. If he is genuine he will wait, but if he is a villain he will disapper by the time you return. Finally, if you do decide that the caller is genuine and let him in never leave him unsupervised alone in a room unless it is totally empty; the fact that someone has a full-time, seemingly respectable job doesn't mean they have no criminal thoughts either.

8
ALARMS

You may think that alarm systems are only available for large houses and industrial and commercial premises and that they are very expensive – neither is the case, and it is possible to provide burglar alarm protection with various levels of sophistication for any home be it a small bed-sit or a large mansion. If you are practically minded you can even do the job yourself, there being a wide range of good DIY alarm kits on the market.

RINGS OF DEFENCE

When considering installing an alarm system it is best to plan rings of defence around your house and its contents. To be really effective you should have more than one ring, starting with a perimeter alarm system to detect someone in the act of breaking in and backing this up with a system of sensors that will detect movement inside the house and around items of particular value.

In most cases off-the-shelf alarm systems will either be specifically for perimeter protection or for movement detection and to gain complete coverage you may have to buy two systems, perhaps even from different manufacturers. However, some systems combine both features and it is often possible to provide both types of protection by adding readily available accessories to the basic kit.

PERIMETER ALARM SYSTEMS

The perimeter alarm system is your first line of defence and is aimed at providing an alarm should anyone attempt to break into the house through a window or door. To be effective it should cover all of the vulnerable outer doors and windows of the house – certainly all the downstairs ones and any upstairs that might be accessible from the roof of a

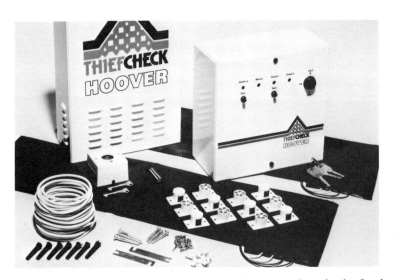

A typical DIY burglar alarm kit – 'hard-wire' system. Can also be fitted professionally.

garage or extension, or by climbing a drainpipe, trellis or nearby tree.

A typical perimeter alarm system would comprise a number of sensors attached to the doors and windows and wired back to a control unit. This, in turn, would be linked to an alarm sounder (usually a bell or siren) mounted on the outside of the house where it can be clearly seen. In addition to, or instead of, the sounder, the control unit might be linked to a remote signalling device that will flash an alarm signal along telephone lines to the police or a central receiving station which, in turn, will alert the appropriate authority. Power for the system is usually taken from the mains via a transformer to reduce the voltage to 12 volts, but standby batteries are also incorporated to maintain the system's integrity in the event of a power cut.

PERIMETER ALARM SENSORS

Magnetic switch
The most common sensor in perimeter alarm systems is the magnetic switch. It comes in two parts; the main body houses a pair of electrical contacts and is fitted to the fixed frame of a door or window; the other part takes the form of a small magnet which is fitted to the moving frame. When

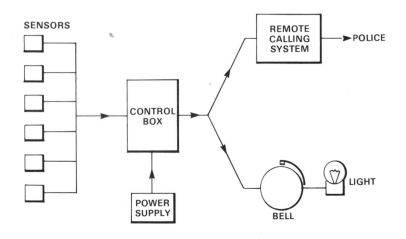

SENSORS

CONTROL BOX

POWER SUPPLY

REMOTE CALLING SYSTEM → POLICE

BELL

LIGHT

A typical burglar alarm circuit – control box is linked to number of sensors, alarm bell and remote calling system (optional).

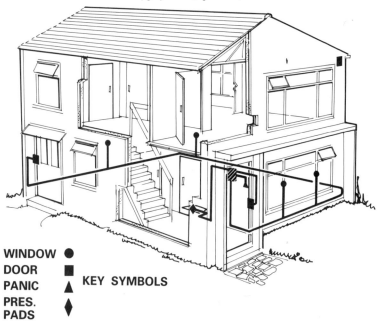

WINDOW ●
DOOR ■
PANIC ▲   KEY SYMBOLS
PRES. PADS ◆

The first house has a single-zone system. The vulnerable entry points on the ground floor should be protected – doors and windows. Also note a pressure pad in the lounge area and panic button by the front door. The delayed exit/entry circuit is on front door contacts.

58

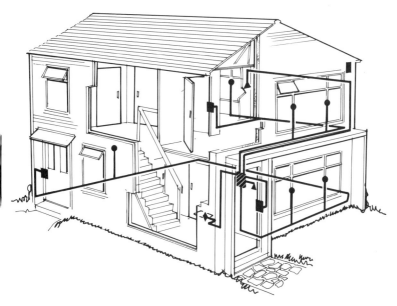

The second house has a twin-zone system and virtually the same layout as the first house on the ground floor with the additional 'switchable' zone covering vulnerable entry points upstairs, and an additional panic button by the bedside.

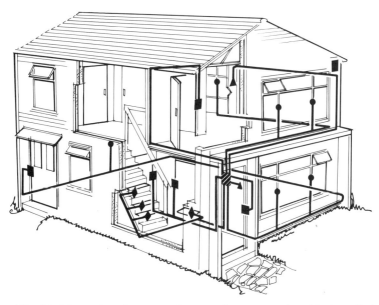

The third house has the same twin-zone alarm system but this time all the exterior vulnerable entry points are protected with the first zone – this can be switched on and you can move around the house – and the second zone on inner doors and pressure pads.

the door or window is closed the magnet holds the switch contacts together, but when the window is opened the magnet no longer affects the contacts and they spring apart to sound the alarm.

Magnetic switches make use of closed-circuit wiring where the switches, the control unit and the wires linking them form a continuous electrical circuit when all the windows and doors protected are closed. If a switch is opened or a wire cut the alarm will sound. Open circuit wiring, which may be used in certain parts of the alarm system, works in the opposite way; in their normal state, the switch contacts are open and will only sound the alarm when closed. The drawback of open circuit wiring in alarm systems is obvious: the thief can cut the wiring anywhere to disable the sensors and the alarm will not sound at all. Having said this, open circuit wiring does have its uses in alarm systems as will be seen later.

The problem with magnetic switches is that they won't prevent a thief from breaking the glass of a large window or glazed door and stepping or crawling through without opening the frame. For this reason it is good practice to conceal the switches as much as possible by fitting them in recesses cut in the frame.

Vibration detector

To overcome the problem of a magnetic sensor not reacting to someone breaking through the window or door rather than breaking it open you can fit a vibration detector. This can be mounted directly to the door or window, or be located on a wall nearby. This type of sensor incorporates a pair of contacts which are kept closed by a weight across them. During the forced entry the vibration caused will topple the weight, the contacts will spring apart and the alarm will sound.

Installation of the vibration detector should be done professionally since it is essential to analyse any vibrations that occur naturally in the building and set the unit's sensitivity so that it won't continually produce false alarms.

Breaking glass detectors

Another method of detecting attacks on the glazed portions of doors and windows is with some form of breaking glass detector, of which there are various types. Two common forms for industrial or commercial use are continuous strips of foil stuck to the glass which break when the glass breaks, or continuous lengths of brittle wire led through aluminium tubes fitted across the window. To get in, the thief must bend the tubes out of the way and this will break the wire inside. In each case the alarm sounds.

There are two types of detector more suitable for domestic use. One is stuck directly to the glass and picks up the vibration as it breaks. The other is an acoustic device which reacts to the sound of the glass breaking.

Personal attack (or panic) button
Another sensor usually provided with a perimeter alarm system is the personal attack or panic button. It is usually recommended that this be mounted near the front door or in the bedroom so that you can raise the alarm instantly should someone try to force their way in past you or somehow manage to get in during the night. In most cases the device will cause the alarm to sound even if the main system is switched off.

A panic button installed by the bedside. Alarm doesn't have to be 'armed' to use. Once used it has to be switched off with key.

ALARM SOUNDERS

There are two popular types of alarm sounder: the bell and the siren, the latter emitting a continuous or modulating high-pitched tone depending on the model. The sounder should be mounted high up on an outside wall so that it cannot be reached easily but can be seen clearly (seeing an alarm sounder will often be enough to put off a thief completely). The sounder will contain its own set of batteries and is linked to the control unit in such a way that even if all the wires are cut the sounder will operate automatically on its own internal power source. The protective cover will also have an anti-tamper device to sound the alarm if an attempt is made to remove it.

Very often the alarm system will be designed to shut off the sounder after about 20 minutes to prevent annoyance to neighbours (particularly if it is a false alarm), but many systems can have a flashing light added to the sounder box which will continue to operate so that police can quickly identify which alarm has been triggered.

REMOTE SIGNALLING DEVICES

If the system is connected directly to a police station or more likely in the case of domestic premises, a central station, it will have a remote signalling device. There are two basic types, both of which use telephone lines to carry their signals (you need to rent a special outgoing-call only line to prevent the signals being blocked by an incoming call).

Automatic dialling equipment (ADE)
When an alarm signal is generated by the system's control unit, the automatic dialling equipment will make an automatic 999 call and relay a pre-recorded message to the police.

Digital communicator
The digital communicator is a much more sophisticated piece of equipment since it can dial the number of its central station more than once until the call is accepted. It then sends a digital coded message to the central station and they will take the appropriate action to contact the police or other

Some alarm systems are based on self-dialling. In an emergency (break-in, fire, illness, etc) pre-set numbers are dialled and emergency message given. Also, like alarm system can be linked to central station facility.

authority depending on the reason for the alarm. It may be a straightforward burglary alarm, or personal attack, or fire, or even a rise in freezer temperature. The coded signal will vary each time.

Both automatic dialling equipment and digital communicators send their messages through the normal public telephone network, but for very high risk situations a direct line is preferable. This will link the system directly with the police station or central station and there is no possibility that a signal will be misrouted, which could happen on the public network. However, the cost of renting a direct line is very expensive, although it can be reduced by a technique known as multiplexing where several people in the same area share the direct line to the central station.

Remote signalling devices are ideal in situations where a house stands on its own well away from other property where a normal alarm sounder may go unnoticed.

CONTROL UNITS

The heart of an alarm system is its control unit. When switched on it monitors the alarm circuits continuously, operating the sounder or remote signalling device immediately it receives a break-in signal.

Control units may be simple or complex depending on the alarm system and the facilities it offers. It will be switched on and off either by a key or a key pad, the latter being more secure since only the owner will know the operating code. It may allow the house to be divided into independently switched alarm zones.

The control unit should provide a separately switched, time-delay circuit to the front door – or whichever main entry/exit point you choose – to allow you to switch the alarm system on and off without triggering it as you come and go. It should have an anti-tamper device built into its cover and have standby batteries to keep the system in operation if the mains power is cut off. It should offer a facility for testing the system and for automatically resetting the system after an alarm has been sounded.

MOVEMENT DETECTION

As with all forms of security when installing alarm systems it is best to plan for the worse and that is why you must build up rings of protection around and inside the house. Although you may have a sophisticated perimeter system, it is as well to take steps to 'trap' thieves with other forms of alarm in case they do somehow manage to get into the house undetected. This is where movement detectors come in, and there are various types to choose from.

Some movement detectors can be linked to the control unit of a perimeter alarm system, but many popular types are completely self-contained with their own power sources and provide individual room protection. They incorporate their own alarm sounders and some even have strobe lights to further alarm and disorientate the burglar. The types of movement detector are listed below.

Pressure mats
The pressure mat is usually an accessory which can be added to a perimeter alarm system and is the one part of the system that will operate on open circuit wiring. The mat comprises two sheets of foil separated by foam with holes cut in it. The foil sheets are linked by wires to the control unit. It is

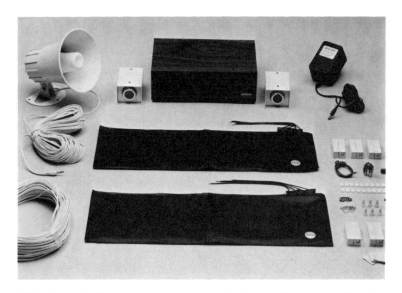

This alarm kit features two pressure pads (centre) these are used under carpet to detect presence. Also internal siren is used.

designed to be laid beneath carpet in areas where a thief is likely to walk – in doorways, on staircases, or in front of valuable items like TVs and video recorders – and when he stands on the mat the two foil sheets make contact and trigger the alarm.

The drawback of the pressure mat is that under thin carpet its outline may show and care must be taken to conceal the wiring to its terminals.

Ultrasonic detector

The ultrasonic movement detector covers a much wider area than a pressure mat and is often difficult to spot since it is common to make it look like a stereo speaker unit. It transmits high frequency sound waves into the room where they are reflected back by all the various surfaces in a definite pattern and this pattern is picked up by a receiver in the unit. If someone enters the room they disrupt the pattern of sound waves, the device recognises the change and triggers the alarm. This change in sound wave pattern is known as the doppler effect. It is quite a reliable way of detecting movement, but it can be affected by turbulent air caused by strong draughts or by the vibrations in the air caused by telephone bells ringing or hissing steam from a kettle.

Microwave detector

Working in a similar manner to the ultrasonic detector, the microwave unit uses high frequency radio waves instead of sound waves. These are unaffected by turbulent air, telephone bells, etc, but they do have other drawbacks. Ultrasonic waves will only fill the room in which the detector is sited, but microwave emissions will actually pass through the walls which means the detector must be positioned carefully to avoid it being triggered by legitimate movement outside the protected room. However, this long-range coverage can be put to good use by protecting the approaches to the room as well as the room itself.

Passive infra-red detector

A fourth type of movement detector is the passive infra-red device (often referred to as a PIR). This operates on a different principle altogether. Unlike the ultrasonic and microwave detectors which actually transmit energy, the PIR simply reads the level of infra-red radiation in the room. If the level changes when someone enters the room for example, it triggers the alarm.

The PIR may be triggered accidentally if a strong shaft of sunlight falls on its sensor or if clouds suddenly obscure the sun. However, it is a relatively cheap form of detector and consumes a very small amount of power.

Used in its own right or additional to alarm system is the 'space detector'. This can use passive infra-red, microwave or ultrasonic. Will detect presence and sound alarm. There are many types on the market to choose from.

Acoustic sensor

It is possible to obtain freestanding acoustic sensors which will listen for the sounds of intruders in a single room or will cover more of the house if doors are left open. Some types make use of remote ultrasonic listening devices that transmit a signal to the control unit when a break-in is detected.

Acoustic sensors share the same problem of microwave detectors in that they can be triggered by perfectly legitimate noises outside the protected area, which could lead to many false alarms.

Combination detectors

Since all the movement detectors have their drawbacks it is possible to obtain units which combine two different methods of detection: microwave and passive infra-red for example. In such a device the drawbacks of one method are compensated for by the other method and vice versa. For an alarm to be sounded, both systems must recognise movement and usually within a specified time limit.

Positioning movement detectors to get the best coverage from them can be a hit and miss affair. However, many have a test light allowing a walk-by test to be made to show the areas of the room where it will respond to an intruder and the areas where it won't. It should be positioned to get the best response, paying particular attention to entry points and valuable items in the room. To get the best from a PIR unit it must be sited using special metering equipment which is able to measure the levels of infra-red radiation in the room.

CENTRAL STATIONS

The advantage of having a link to a central station is that someone actually keeps an eye on your property continuously whether you are at home or away, albeit with the aid of electronics. Various security firms operate central stations throughout the country, the object being to provide a facility for monitoring alarm systems 24 hours a day, 365 days a year. Not only do they respond to burglaries but also personal distress, fire and other events that can cause problems when you are away – a freezer breakdown for example. On receipt of an alarm signal they will notify the appropriate authority, or someone nominated by you.

CHOOSING AN ALARM SYSTEM

There is a wide range of alarm systems for DIY installation and choosing the right one can be difficult; it is easy to get carried away with over-sophistication with the risk of ending up with a system that is too complex to be used easily. That means you will be less likely to use it regularly which defeats the object of having a system in the first place.

Unfortunately, there is no standard by which you can judge the equipment, although there is a British Standard that covers complete professional installations (BS4737). This has no application to DIY systems at all, however. As a guide, make sure any system you buy meets the following requirements:

1. The system should operate from a mains electricity supply with a standby battery power source in case of mains failure. The batteries should be rechargeable and there should be some form of battery condition indicator to warn when battery voltage is low before it drops to a level where it would be unable to operate the alarm system.

2. The external alarm sounder should be self activated in case the link from the control unit is cut or it is wrenched from the wall. The cover should incorporate an anti-tamper device.

3. Any remote signalling device must be self-contained and protected by a secure housing. It should have its own battery so that it can send a signal even if the power supply is cut off.

4. All parts of the system which can affect its efficiency must be fitted with anti-tamper devices to sound the alarm if they are attacked.

5. There should be a test facility so that you can check the system before switching it on.

6. You should be able to switch the system on and leave the house without triggering it; similarly, when you return home, there should be time for you to reach the control unit and switch the alarm off before it sounds.

In addition, the system should match your needs by providing the correct number and type of sensors for both perimeter protection and movement detection. You may also want to include smoke detectors or sensors to monitor freezer temperature, etc. Consider the options carefully, compare prices and decide which suits you best.

Obviously, if you intend having a professionally installed system, you can have it tailored to meet your needs exactly.

INSTALLING DIY BURGLAR ALARMS

Many manufacturers, including some well-known names in the domestic appliance field, have cottoned on to the fact that there is a very great demand for DIY security systems and burglar alarms in particular. The result is that you can now install an alarm system yourself for a relatively small outlay – £200 or £300 at the most. In most cases they are perimeter systems with additional accessories available such as pressure pads to provide a degree of movement detection inside the house as well.

The first thing to do is look at your house and imagine how you will divide it up into protected zones. If only one zone is available it is probably best to cover all the downstairs windows and outer doors with the addition of a personal attack button near the front door and a pressure mat in front of some valuable item (a video recorder, for example). If two zones are available you could split the upstairs windows and the downstairs windows and doors into the two zones, or put all the windows and outer doors on one zone and use the other for movement detection with switches on inner doors, pressure mats, etc. The zones should be independently controlled so that you can switch off the inner movement detection system when you are home during the day yet leave the perimeter system switched on.

Installing the equipment is quite straightforward and kits will include all the necessary sensors, control unit, alarm sounder and wiring. They will often supply mounting screws, wall plugs and cable clips as well. Sensors are screwed to wooden door and window frames or stuck to metal frames using self adhesive pads. Wherever possible the sensors should be set in recesses cut in the frames to disguise their presence and the wiring led to them through holes drilled in the frames. The wiring should be clipped unobtrusively along skirting boards, in the angles of wooden frames, and run under carpets out of sight. Alternatively, it can be buried in the wall or run in thin conduit. By fitting sensors at the bottoms of door and window frames less wire will be needed to reach them.

Ideally, the control unit should be mounted out of the way in a cupboard where it won't be immediately noticed by callers to the house. It should be connected to the mains electricity supply through a fused connection unit rather than a plug and socket. Don't, however, run the alarm system wiring close to any mains electrical wiring as the latter could be the source of false alarms.

When mounting the sounder outside, make sure it is high up on a wall and inaccessible, but it must be easily seen so that it acts as a deterrent. At the same time, keep it as close to the control unit position as posible to reduce the length of the connecting wiring run. The personal attack button should also be mounted out of the reach of children to avoid the possibility of false alarms; always keep its resetting key in the same place so you can get to it quickly.

PROFESSIONAL INSTALLATIONS

There is not doubt that having an alarm system professionally installed will cost you a lot more than if you did it yourself using a proprietary alarm kit – perhaps three or four times as much. However, there are certain advantages to employing a professional installer, one being that you will get a system designed to meet your needs and premises exactly. No matter how good the system, this is something that the DIY alarm cannot always do. Every situation will be different: the structure of the house, its location, the kind of protection required, the habits of the owners – all have to be taken into account when designing the system.

Professionally installed systems offer a much wider scope in the type of protection available – a system linked to a central station, for example, must be professionally installed – and any installer worth his salt will offer a 24-hour emergency repair service and a regular maintenance contract. Another advantage of the professionally installed system is that it is often possible to obtain a discount on insurance premiums as a result of the installation – as much as 25 per cent in some instances.

A start in tracking down bona fide alarm installers is to check with your local Crime Prevention Officer. He can tell

you the sort of system you need and should be able to give
you the names of installers in your area. Another way is to
contact the National Supervisory Council For Intruder Alarms
(NSCIA) who will provide a list of their member companies
(their address appears on page 95). To gain NSCIA approval a member company must be able to show experience
in installing and servicing alarm equipment, must have suitable premises, tools, plant and stock to render an efficient
24-hour emergency and maintenance service, be in a sound
financial and commercial position, and install and service
systems in accordance with the requirements of BS4737.

Something to be aware of is the fact that purchasing a
professionally installed alarm system may bring with it an
obligation to enter into a maintenance contract for a specified number of years and this obviously means more expense. Depending on the equipment used, this may mean
two regular checks each year or possibly more if it is really
complex.

Many perfectly reliable companies may not be NSCIA
members and here you will not really know what kind of
service to expect. You are likely to be safe with the big, well
known security companies, but if the name is unknown to
you ask the installer to supply you with the names and
addresses of two or three recent customers so that you can
ask their opinion of the service provided. Alternatively, you
can find an installer by asking people living nearby who may
have already had systems put in.

AVOIDING FALSE ALARMS

Early alarm systems were, and still are, a real nuisance when
triggered accidentally since they will continue to sound until
the system is switched off, and if the owner is away on
holiday for two weeks that is a very long time! Even over-
night can be trying. Fortunately, modern alarms have sounders
that switch themselves off after a certain period (about 20
minutes), the alarm system usually rearming itself at the
same time. Some may also have a flashing light which will
continue to operate after the sounder has switched itself off
to aid police in locating it.

Of course, the alarm may have been triggered by a thief
who ran away on hearing the noise, you may never know,

but if the alarm is not switched off and reset immediately it will soon lose you any friends you may have among your neighbours. To minimise this problem it is best to leave a key to your house with a trustworthy neighbour or a relative when you are away, and tell the police where they can be reached if necessary. Make sure the person you leave the key with knows how to switch off the system, and reset it.

If you have a system linked to a central station and you trigger it accidentally, phone them immediately and let them know. They will probably call you back to verify that it is a false alarm, but at least you will have acted responsibly.

Making sure the system is properly installed and operated will go a long way to avoiding false alarms, and whether you install the system yourself or have it done professionally it is a good idea to make the following checks:

1. All the fittings in the system must be securely mounted using fixings suitable for the surface they are mounted to.

2. The wiring should be neatly routed and well clipped to prevent sagging wires that might catch in a vacuum cleaner or be snagged when moving furniture.

3. Where cable is connected to the terminals of fittings, make sure it is securely located beneath the terminal washer with no stray whisker of wire poking out to short circuit on adjacent terminals. Make sure the terminals are tight.

4. All wiring connections must be made at proper terminals or be soldered joints. Any wires just twisted together to make a connection will eventually oxidise and cause an increase in electrical resistance which can cause a false alarm.

5. Wire to wire joints should be sealed with insulating tape or a proper insulating sleeve to prevent short circuits.

6. Where cables enter fittings through holes in their casings, a grommet should be fitted to the hole to prevent the cables chafing on the edge of the hole.

7. Cables should not be run alongside mains electrical cables; the current surges in the mains cables cause inductive transfer from one cable to the other and with it a false alarm.

8. The system should not take its power from a 13 amp socket which is also used for other purposes. It is quite possible that someone will forget to plug the system back in and the standby battery will exhaust itself, causing the

sounder to signal an alarm. The best form of power connection is an unswitched fused connector unit.

9. Doors and windows fitted with magnetic switches must be a good fit in their frames and secured properly so that they cannot rattle in the wind or be vibrated sufficiently to open the switch contacts. If the switch is installed on a metal frame the magnetism might be diverted. Always check to see that the switch contacts are held firmly closed by the magnet and do not drop open after a few operations or with vibration.

10. Pressure mats must not be installed on a damp floor or rest on any sharp objects. They should be secured to the floor so that they cannot wander and strain the cable connections.

11. PIR sensors must be positioned so that shafts of sunlight or the beams from car headlamps cannot fall upon them. Do not leave a tungsten lamp burning in the room protected by a PIR; if the lamp burns out it will trigger an alarm.

12. Ultrasonic detectors must be placed clear of strong draughts and away from telephones; both can trigger an alarm.

13. Read and make sure you fully understand the operating instructions supplied with the alarm system.

There are also certain steps you can take when using your alarm system to prevent accidental false alarms. These are as follows:

1. Close and latch all protected doors and windows securely before setting the alarm system.

2. Don't place any item of furniture on top of a pressure mat; after a while the weight of the piece will gradually flatten the mat until the contacts meet.

3. Don't leave anything balanced precariously in an area covered by a movement detector. If it should fall later it will trigger an alarm.

4. Before you set the alarm, make sure no one is left in any of the protected areas.

5. Don't leave pets free to roam areas protected by movement or vibration detectors.

6. When leaving for a holiday, make sure the electricity supply to the alarm system has not been cut off accidentally by the removal of a plug or a switch that has been turned off.

7. Once you have set the alarm, don't stray from the designed exit route to collect something you have forgotten (a briefcase, umbrella, etc).

8. Some systems are set by turning the key in a shunt lock on the front door. Don't turn the key while the door is open; when you turn the key to withdraw the bolt so that you can close the door, the alarm will sound.

9. If the system offers a timed exit, make sure you leave the house before the time expires.

10. When you return to the house, go straight to the control unit along the designed entry route and switch the system off.

LOOKING AFTER THE ELDERLY

Panic buttons are an essential accessory to any alarm system fitted in an old person's home, so that if necessary they can summon help with the aid of the alarm system. Unfortunately, the problem with most panic buttons is that they are permanent fixtures linked by wires to the system's control unit. Even if a button was to be put in every room in the house, they might not provide the help expected of them. A serious fall could leave a victim immobile, unable to reach the button that could bring help, and what if the fall was to occur at the bottom of the garden?

Fortunately, it is possible to obtain self-contained panic button radio transmitters which can be worn round the neck as a pendant. They send a signal to a remote signalling device which, in turn, can summon aid through a central station. Some signalling devices will also dial other numbers (of relatives, doctors, etc) and relay a taped message.

In a dangerous situation, due to illness or some form of attack by an intruder in or around the house, all the wearer has to do is operate the switch and the signal it transmits will raise the alarm – even if the main alarm system is turned off.

These remote control devices will usually operate up to 100 metres from the control unit, which can also be used to control a complete alarm system. Some units take the place of a standard telephone, having a handset and dialling facility as well.

PERSONAL ATTACK ALARMS

Up to now only home-based fixed alarm systems have been considered but one hears constantly of muggings and attacks on people in the street, the elderly and women being favourite victims. To combat the thugs who perpetrate these crimes it is possible to choose from a wide range of personal alarms. These usually give off a high-pitched shrieking sound which should be enough to startle an attacker and make him run off, at the same time drawing attention of other people to your plight.

All of these personal alarms are small enough to carry in a pocket or handbag, but the best are designed to be worn round the neck as a pendant or on the wrist where they are immediately accessible – there may not always be time to fumble in a handbag for the alarm if the attack is sudden and vicious. When buying one of these small alarms, look for one that will continue to operate even if dropped.

ALARM SYSTEM GLOSSARY

When shopping for an alarm system, you may come across all manner of unfamiliar terms manufacturers use to describe their products. The following glossary will help you understand what those terms mean:

Acoustic detector – a sensor that listens for the sounds of a break-in (broken glass, etc).

Alarm sounder – usually a bell or siren mounted high on an outside wall which is set off when the system's control unit detects a break-in. It will have its own power system and will sound if the wires to it are cut or if it is pulled from the wall.

Anti-tamper device – a small switch built into the casing of an alarm control unit, sounder or remote signalling device which triggers the alarm if an attempt is made to open the casing.

Automatic dialling equipment – a remote signalling device which will automatically make a 999 call to the police and relay them a pre-recorded message to indicate a break-in.

Beam interruption – a system of infra-red invisible light beams projected across likely entry ways. When the beam is broken by someone walking through it the alarm is triggered. Not common for domestic alarm systems.

Breaking glass detector – a sensor fitted to the glazed portion of a door or window to detect the vibrations caused if the glass is broken. Acoustic sensors may also be used for this purpose.

Central station – a 24-hour monitoring service linked to your alarm system. When the system is triggered, it sends a signal over telephone lines to the central station where the operator will contact the appropriate authority (police, fire service, ambulance, etc). He may also contact relatives or a doctor if an elderly person is involved.

Control unit – heart of the alarm system, receiving signals from the various sensor devices and operating the alarm sounder and/or remote signalling device.

Digital communicator – a remote signalling device which sends a digital code to a central station to indicate the location of an alarm and the reason for the alarm.

Direct line system – a private telephone line link to a police station or more probably a central station. More expensive than using the public telephone network but much more reliable.

Hard-wire system – an alarm system (usually perimeter type) which uses thin wires to connect the various sensors, control unit and alarm sounder.

Magnetic switch – a sensor for fitting to doors and windows which will trigger the alarm if the door or window is forced open.

Microwave sensor – a movement detector which transmits high frequency radio waves which are reflected in a certain pattern by the various surfaces in the room and received back by the unit. Any change in the pattern caused by someone entering the room will trigger the alarm.

Movement detectors – sensors designed to detect movement inside a house (acoustic, microwave, passive infra-red, pressure mat, ultrasonic). Won't sound the alarm until the intruder has actually broken in. Often self-contained units which provide protection only for the room in which they are sited. Easily installed, but best teamed with a perimeter alarm system.

Panic button – linked into a hard-wire system and usually sited next to the front door or in the bedroom. When pressed it sounds the alarm instantly even if the main system is switched off. Remote radio transmitter panic buttons also available for wearing round the neck as a pendant – ideal for the elderly.

Passive infra-red sensor – a movement detector which measures the level of infra-red radiation in a room. Any change in the level of radiation caused by someone entering the room will trigger the alarm.

Perimeter alarm system – an alarm system with sensors fitted to the outer doors and windows of the house which will sound if an attempt is made to break in.

Personal attack button – see **Panic button.**

Pressure mat – a movement detector for laying beneath carpets where a thief is likely to tread (hallways, doorways, stairs, etc) and also in front of valuable items such as TVs and video recorders. When stood on the contacts close and the alarm sounds. It is installed as part of a hard-wire system.

Remote signalling device – automatic dialling equipment or digital communicator which sends a silent alarm signal to a police station or more probably a central station. It makes use of the public telephone network (a separate outgoing-call only line should be rented) or a direct line link.

Ultrasonic sensor – a movement detector which transmits high frequency sound waves (too high for the human ear) which are reflected in a certain pattern by the various surfaces in the room and received back by the unit. Any change in the pattern caused by someone entering the room will trigger the alarm.

Vibration detector – a perimeter alarm sensor for fitting to a window or door, or nearby, to pick up the vibrations caused by an attack on the structure of the window or door.

9
INSURANCE

It is estimated that some 25 per cent of all householders in Britain have no insurance cover for the contents of their homes, and of the remaining 75 per cent most do not have adequate cover. It is surprising just how much property you can accumulate over the years; imagine the disaster if most of it was destroyed in a major fire and you were faced with replacing everything out of your own pocket. If you were to price every item in your house with its current retail value you would be in for quite a shock.

Of course, you may already have an insurance policy to cover your possessions but is it up to date? Do you religiously increase the sum insured every time you buy something new? How often do you make a check that you have the right amount of cover? An insurance policy of this kind cannot be simply tucked away and forgotten; it must be continually appraised and uprated if you are not to be faced with dipping into your savings or going without certain items in the event of a claim.

REBUILDING COSTS

There are two types of insurance cover for your home and possessions: one covers the cost of rebuilding the structure (including outbuildings such as garages and sheds) and the other provides for the repair or replacement of the contents. Of the two, the former is the cover most likely to be held by most home owners for the simple reason that building societies insist on it as a condition of granting a mortgage. It is usually arranged through the society at the time of buying the house, although many societies are becoming more amenable to the buyer arranging his own insurance with the company of his choice.

The premium for buildings insurance is usually calculated at the same rate (about 15p for every £100 insured) throughout the country. However, if the house is of non-standard construction (timber framed, or with a thatched roof, for example) this must be declared to the insurers who will probably charge a higher premium because certain risks, such as fire, may be greater than normal. It is worth looking around, though, as some companies are quoting advantageous terms in respect of certain types of house and considerable savings in premium can be made if your house falls into the right category.

The drawback of most forms of buildings insurance is that you have to estimate the sum insured yourself and if you get this figure wrong it can have serious consequences. If the sum insured is too low not only will you not have enough to rebuild the house completely should this ever be required, but it may also mean that any claim you make (however small it may be) will result in a settlement that is reduced in proportion to the amount by which you were under insured. On the other hand, if you over estimate the rebuilding costs, the sum insured will be higher than necessary and you will be wasting money by paying too high a premium.

Fortunately, some insurance companies are now offering buildings insurance that does not require you to specify a sum insured, the premium being related to the floor area of the house, or it may be based on the type of house and its locality. In the event of a claim, the full rebuilding costs will be met and you need not worry about getting your sums right!

If you are not required by a building society to effect an insurance policy through them or with a particular company, it is as well to seek the advice of an insurance broker who should be able to get you the best cover at the most advantageous terms. There will be no charge to you for this service; he is paid a fee by the company with whom he places the business.

COVERING THE HOUSE CONTENTS

Like buildings insurance, a contents policy can be arranged to provide cover for 'specified perils' or for 'all risks', but in the latter case the premium is likely to be considerably higher. You may also have to pay an extra premium with an all risks policy if any particularly valuable items exceed a specified percentage of the total sum insured.

The specified perils policy will give only limited coverage to the kind of possessions that are regularly taken away from the house – jewellery, fur coats, cameras, sports gear and the like – but it is often possible to arrange all risks coverage on these specific items whether they are in the house or outside.

Valuable items of jewellery will have to be listed separately on the proposal form together with the value of each piece, and for particularly valuable pieces the insurers may ask for a professional valuation. In any case, it is always useful to have some proof of an item's value, particularly if it is unique and cannot be compared with anything else for the purposes of settling a claim. Always keep receipts. You should also notify the insurers of any other items of value you may possess: works of art, collections, etc.

The sum insured will vary depending on the type of policy; one type reflects the true current value of all your possessions taking into account depreciation due to their age and fair wear and tear; the other sets out to replace items on a 'new for old' basis (with the exception usually of household linen and clothes).

The former is the traditional way of arranging this type of insurance and with it, in the event of a claim, you would be paid a percentage of the new cost of the item being claimed for. As an example, it is generally reckoned that the life of a portable TV is 15 years, so if you were claiming for replacement of a set that was five years old, you would only receive ⅔ of its replacement value. When specifying the sum insured under this type of policy, you have to take into account the current 'used' value of everything you own and obviously it must be updated at each renewal date.

Such cover is all very well in that it reflects the true value of your possessions, but it doesn't necessarily help in replacing them since you cannot always find secondhand substitutes to match the condition of the originals, and trying to obtain secondhand curtains and carpets would be very difficult. This led insurers to introduce the new for old policy. With this type of cover you must make sure that the sum insured reflects the value of your property based on its replacement cost, and you will be very surprised just how much this can be.

DISCOUNTS ON PREMIUMS

Where the contents of a house are covered by an all risks policy, the insurer will probably require the policy holder to pay the first £25 of any claim. Sometimes the size of this excess can earn a discout on the premium – up to 20 per cent if the excess is £100 or more.

Discounts on premiums can often be gained by other means; many companies will give a discount if the house has a professionally installed burglar alarm system. Some may even be prepared to give a small discount for a DIY system. However, if the company itself has insisted on the installation of an alarm there will be no discount as the existence of the alarm is a condition of the company accepting the risk at all.

MAKING A CLAIM

If you should make a claim under one of these policies, the insurers may appoint an independent loss adjuster to recommend a figure for settlement, but if you would like someone to put your case for you – someone who speaks the insurance company's language – you can employ a public loss assessor yourself. If the claim is substantial – £2,000 or more – he may charge 10 per cent of the claim plus VAT and this fee must come out of your pocket; it cannot form part of the claim.

10
SAFETY IN THE HOME

Protecting yourself at home is just as important as protecting your property – not just from attack by intruders but also from injury or worse caused by accidents. It is a sobering thought that over 6,500 accidental deaths occur in the home every year, not to mention over 80,000 serious injuries. Most of these could be avoided by the application of a little commonsense and by taking a few simple precautions.

When people go to work their employers are bound by the Health and Safety at Work Act to provide a safe working environment, and employees are required to co-operate to ensure that accidents don't happen. This legislation can even extend to your home if you are self-employed or run a business from home. If you don't, however, there is no legal requirement for you to provide yourself and your family with a safe environment to live in, other than a basic Occupiers Liability. This is aimed at protecting visitors or anyone who may be on your property and who suffers injury as a result of your negligence – by a tile falling from a roof, for example.

Cooking, household chores, DIY activities are all things we do every day and they are all potentially hazardous. Yet very few take even the simplest of precautions to prevent an accident happening. The safety consciousness and responsibility learnt in the workplace is seldom brought into the home; if it was the number of accidents could be reduced considerably. Commonsense plays a major part in preventing accidents.

SAFETY IN THE KITCHEN

The kitchen is a particularly dangerous place with sharp cutting tools, naked flames, red hot electric elements, boil-

82

ing water, steam and extremely hot fats and oils. Loose mats or children's toys can cause you to stumble, and the inquisitive fingers of youngsters can lead to horrific burns and scalds.

Many injuries are caused by sharp instruments like knives, choppers and saws, but a little care in their use could prevent these happening. Always use a proper cutting board or chopping block and make sure the tool does not have a greasy handle or a blunt blade. When you clean any tool with a cutting edge, always wash it separately with the blade pointing downwards away from you.

Domestic appliances often have safety devices built into them but even so accidents can happen, so make sure they are maintained in accordance with the maker's instructions, particularly infra-red and microwave cookers – exposure to their radiation can be a health hazard. Steam can also cause nasty injuries, so treat kettles, pressure cookers and pans with respect. Pressure can build up inside food tins and it is a wise precaution to drape a tea towel over a tin before you pierce it with the tin opener.

PREVENTING BACK INJURIES

When lifting anything from a low level there are some simple rules to follow to avoid damaging your back or your stomach. Stand in front of the object with your feet slightly apart and bend your knees until you are in a squatting position. Grip the object and keeping your chin in and your back as straight as possible straighten your legs until you are standing upright. Never keep your legs straight and bend at the waist to pick up something from a low level; this is a recipe for disaster. Once on the move, keep the object as close to you as possible and make sure you can see where you are going.

SAFETY WITH LADDERS

Falls from ladders also cause many injuries, often injuries that could be avoided. Ladders will topple easily if they are not secured properly and a hazard with wooden ladders is improper or a total lack of maintenance leading to failure when you stand on them.

When you lean a ladder against a wall, make sure the foot of the ladder is 1 ft away from the wall for every 4 ft in height. Tie the foot of the ladder to stakes driven into the ground, or on soft ground support its feet on a wooden board secured by stakes. When the ladder is extended to a considerable height tie the top to a batten spanning the inside of a window frame or to eyebolts driven into the wall. Never lean the ladder on a gutter and make sure the top extends at least $3\frac{1}{2}$ ft above the upper resting point.

Never be tempted to over–reach from a ladder; it's surprising how many people, keen to finish a job, will stretch out too far and overbalance. Always move the ladder along, even if the job does take longer.

If you intend working on a roof, make sure you have a safety harness, plenty of securing points, suitable ladders and crawling boards. Watch out for insecure gutters, loose roof tiles and children playing below.

WORKING WITH ELECTRICITY

Faulty wiring and electrical appliances can cause fires (see below) and serious injury or even death if you are unlucky enough to receive an electric shock. Extreme care is needed whenever any electrical work is carried out and if you are at all unsure of what you are doing, call in a professional electrician.

TAKING CARE WITH GLASS

Glass is an attractive and versatile product which surrounds us in windows, doors, furniture and the like, and we tend to take it for granted. Yet glass is responsible for injuring around 25,000 people every year in accidents around the home. Because ordinary glass is so easily broken, it is often the criminal's means of entry, too. So you can see that the glass in your home deserves particular attention to ensure both the safety of yourself and family and the security of your possessions.

There are various types of glass available for domestic use, including special safety types, and by choosing the most appropriate type for the job it has to do, you will reduce the likelihood of injury if it is broken.

Ordinary or annealed glass – This is the most common form of glass (variations are sheet, float, plate, figure rolled and obscured). It is very brittle and will shatter into sharp, jagged pieces under a sudden blow.

Toughened glass – Also known as tempered glass, this is made by heat treating annealed glass to make it up to five times stronger. If it does break under a violent impact, it will shatter into thousands of tiny, relatively harmless, pieces. You may well have seen a car windscreen broken in this way.

Laminated glass – This is of sandwich construction, two thin layers of annealed glass being bonded to a thin middle layer of plastic. Under violent impact, the glass panel will remain in one piece, the plastic middle layer holding the sharp fragments of glass together. In many countries it is compulsory for cars to have laminated windscreens, and it is becoming increasingly common on British-built cars.

Wired glass – This is made by embedding a wire mesh into annealed glass when it is made. Although the glass will crack under a blow, the wire will hold the pieces together.

REDUCING THE RISKS FROM GLASS

One obvious way of keeping the risks from broken glass to a minimun would be to replace all the glass in the house with safety glass. However, this would be expensive and in many areas unnecessary. Safety glass is essential in some areas of the house, though. Before discussing these, it would be as well to give some guidelines as to the way glass should be treated in general to prevent accidents.

1. Use a simple barrier or low–level sill to protect low level windows.
2. Protect fixed glass panels next to doors and windows by rails or screen them with furniture, flower displays, etc.
3. Stop children larking about near any glazed areas of the house.
4. Make all glass doors and panels obvious by marking them with some form of motif or decoration.

5. Make sure all glazed areas are well lit at night.
6. Where transparent glass is not essential, use opaque or obscured glass which will be more visible.
7. When opening a door or window, never push on the glass and never strike the glass to free a jammed door or window.
8. Don't bang on glass to attract someone's attention and never hit it in temper. Avoid slamming doors and windows.
9. Don't place loose rugs or mats anywhere near glass.
10. If any glass does get broken, sweep up the pieces immediately and wrap them carefully before throwing them away. If pieces are too large to sweep up, wear thick gloves to pick them up.

THE DANGERS OF FIRE

The fire brigade attends at least 50,000 fires in dwellings every year; hundreds of people die in those fires, and thousands more are injured. Yet many of these deaths and injuries need not happen if the right precautions are taken to prevent fire breaking out in the first place. Knowing the danger areas and the likely reasons for a fire breaking out will give you an idea of how they may be prevented. Common sources of fire are smokers' materials and matches; heating appliances, particularly electric fires; solid fuel fires and mains gas fires; electrical equipment such as blankets and cookers; electrical wiring; and gas cookers.

Fires occur most frequently in the kitchen, often due to pans of fat or oil catching fire. However, most fire deaths usually occur in a living room or bedroom from fires involving clothing, upholstery or bedding and usually the victim has direct contact with the source of ignition. Often the victims are the elderly or infirm.

The likely dangers are listed on the following pages and you should study these closely together with the rest of your family so that you all understand the dangers.

For all the areas of risk there are precautions you can take to minimise the likelihood of fire breaking out:

Smoking
* Every room in which people smoke must have ashtrays.

* Extinguish all matches, cigarettes and pipes immediately after use in an ashtray; don't drop them on a chair, the carpet or into a wastepaper basket.
* Never leave a lighted cigarette on the edge of an ashtray or anywhere where it might fall off on to the carpet or a chair.
* Do not smoke in bed or for at least an hour before going to bed so that you are sure nothing is left smouldering.
* If you really must smoke in bed, give serious consideration to using flame-retardent bedding; many people have been killed by going off to sleep and dropping a cigarette on to the bed covers.
* Never empty ashtrays into a wastepaper basket.
* Before you go to bed, check the house to make sure nothing is left smouldering.

Heating
* Never hang clothing in front of a fire, or drape it over a heater to dry.

Take the following precautions with a radiant gas fire:
* Fix it firmly to the wall.
* Make sure it has a guard conforming to the British Standard.
* It should have a pilot light or spark ignition.
* Only use it in a well ventilated room.

The following apply to electric radiant heaters, LPG radiant heaters and oil fired convector heaters:
* Make sure they comply with the relevant British Standard and have suitable guards.
* Keep them clean and well maintained.
* Stand them away from any combustible materials such as curtains, clothing, furniture, bedding, paper and children's toys.
* Stand them where they are unlikely to be knocked over.
* Never link them to a timeswitch or thermostat controller since the heater may come on when you are out.

In addition with an oil-fired convector heater:
* Fix it firmly to a wall or floor, making sure it is level.
* The room should be well ventilated but not draughty.
* Whenever possible fill the paraffin container out of doors.

* Never move or fill the heater when it is alight.
* Keep paraffin in plastic or metal containers with screw tops, preferably out of doors in an outhouse. If there is no alternative to keeping it indoors, limit the amount to 23 litres (5 gallons), making sure it is stored in a cool place well away from any source of ignition.

With a solid-fuel fire:
* Never use flammable liquids like petrol or paraffin to light it.
* Never hold a sheet or newspaper or similar combustible material in front of the fireplace to 'draw' the fire.
* Never leave the fire unguarded when there is no one in the room. Guard the fire at all times if there are elderly or very young people in the house.
* Never carry hot coals from one room to another.
* Have a metal bin, preferably with a close fitting lid, by the fireside for the ashes before carrying them outside.
* Damp down the fire before going to bed.
* Have the chimney swept at least twice a year.
* Don't hang a mirror over a fireplace or place anything that a child might want on the mantelshelf.
* If you think the chimney is on fire, call the fire brigade at once. Remove the hearth rug or any other materials that could catch fire.

Electricity
* Regularly check flexes on all electrical appliances, replacing them immediately they show the slightest sign of wear or damage.
* Never join flex by merely twisting the inner cores together; if a joint is necessary, use a proper insulated connector until a new single length of flex can be fitted.
* Never run flex near hot surfaces or naked flames, or under carpets where it can wear dangerously and not be noticed.
* Never cover a light bulb with paper or fabric.
* Make sure you have enough socket outlets for your needs without having to use long trailing leads or multi-way adaptors.
* Make sure fuses are always of the correct rating for the job they are to do, and never be tempted to replace a fuse

that keeps blowing with one of a higher rating. Have an electrician find the reason for the constantly blowing fuse.

* Have the wiring in your house checked every five years by a qualified electrician.
* Never use electrical appliances that are obviously faulty.
* Never run an iron or any other electrical appliance from a light bulb socket.
* Switch off and unplug all electrical appliances, particularly irons, TVs and radios, when not in use or if there is a power failure. In the latter case, the power may come on when you are out or in bed.

With electric blankets:
* Always unplug an underblanket before you get into bed unless it is marked as being suitable for all-night use.
* Never use an underblanket as an overblanket and vice versa.
* Fold the blanket carefully without creasing it when not in use.
* Send it back to the makers every three years for servicing unless they recommend a more frequent interval.
* Make sure the blanket carries a label showing that it complies with BS 3456. If it does not conform to this standard throw it away.

Cooking
* Never lean over a hob unit when a gas ring is alight or a hotplate switched on.
* Fill fat pans to no more than half their depth and never leave them unattended. If you have to leave the room, turn off the heat.
* Always dry chips before putting them into hot fat or oil.
* Never place tea towels over the cooker, or hang them on the oven door, to dry.
* Don't decorate the kitchen ceiling with expanded polystyrene tiles, and if they are already fitted never paint them with an oil-based paint.

Mains gas and bottled gas appliances
Both mains and bottled gas (LPG) can asphyxiate a person and will readily form an explosive mixture when mixed with air.

* Provide good ventilation to the room where any gas appliance is sited.

* If the gas burner does not light up almost immediately when you turn on the gas, turn it off again and check that the pilot light is lit or that the ignition device is working.

* If you smell gas, extinguish all possible sources of ignition – cigarettes, naked flames, electric fires, etc. Open doors and windows to disperse the gas and check that no pilot light has gone out or a gas tap has been left turned on. If neither is the case, the cause is probably a leak. With mains gas, turn off the supply at the meter and call a gas service engineer; with a bottled gas appliance, disconnect the bottle and place it outside. Then have the appliance checked by an engineer.

* Check that gas taps which are in reach of children cannot be knocked on easily; the best type to use has a removable key which should be kept out of reach of youngsters. With bottled gas appliances:

* Whenever possible change LPG cylinders outdoors; otherwise provide plenty of ventilation by opening windows and doors.

* Make sure both the cylinder taps are fully off before changing them over.

* If cylinder connection involves tightening a nut, turn it just enough to ensure a gas-tight seal but do not overtighten.

* With a self-sealing connector, make sure the regulator or adaptor is turned off before connecting. Never remove the regulator while the heater is still alight.

* Always replace the safety cap on the cylinder valve when it is not in use or when it is empty.

* Keep spare cylinders in an outhouse if at all possible. If they must be kept indoors, store them in a safe place well away from any source of ignition.

* Make sure all flexible hoses used with bottled gas equipment comply with the requirements of BS 3212.

Other precautions
* Never leave children alone in the house.
* Keep matches and cigarette lighters away from children, and always use safety matches.
* Many aerosols contain flammable liquids and should be marked to this effect. However, it is as well to keep all

aerosols away from naked flames or hot surfaces and never smoke while using them. Never put empty aerosol cans on a fire. Whenever possible use non-flammable cleaning agents.

* Never use petrol in the house for any purpose.
* Never allow waste paper and rubbish to accumulate, particularly in cupboards, lofts and cellars.
* Keep magnifying mirrors used for shaving out of direct sunlight.
* Never use candles for lighting.
* Insulate the loft with non-flammable materials.
* Never use a naked flame for light in the loft – use a torch.
* Keep the hallway and stairs clear of obstruction at all times.
* In flats and maisonettes keep the doors leading to communal stairways closed at all times.
* Fit a substantial metal box with a lid to the letterbox.
* Last thing at night: switch off and remove the plug of every electrical appliance not in use; turn off portable heaters and make sure open fires are in safe condition and well guarded; make sure all cigarettes and pipes have been extinguished properly; check each room to ensure that everything is in order; close all ground floor doors and windows.

Furniture
* When buying new furniture make sure it carries labels to indicate that the upholstery materials comply with the Upholstered Furniture (Safety) Regulations 1980 and the Upholstered Furniture (Safety) (Amendment) Regulations 1983.

FAMILY FIRE DRILL

A fire breaking out with its attendant smoke and heat can disorientate people and cause them to panic and this may lead them to become trapped when they might otherwise escape. So pre-planning your moves in the event of a fire will save you vital seconds and reduce the feeling of panic. Discuss what you should do with the other members of your family and go over the fire drill regularly so that it is not forgotten.

When a fire is discovered that cannot be extinguished immediately and safely:
* Raise the alarm, by yelling 'FIRE'.

*   Evacuate everyone from the house, closing doors as you go.
*   Call the fire brigade from a neighbour's telephone or a callbox. If the house is semi-detached or terraced, evacuate neighbours from adjoining properties.

When working out your fire drill:
*   Imagine a fire starting in each room of the house in turn and decide which escape route you would use in each case. Whenever possible, evacuate the house through the front door.
*   Young children, the elderly or infirm will probably need help during evacuation. Disabled people should have ground-floor bedrooms whenever possible.
*   If there is a lot of smoke, the air will be clearer near the floor so it is safest to crawl along.
*   Make sure you can open the front door easily; if a key is required to operate the lock on the inside make sure it is kept where it can be reached quickly.
*   Once outside, keep a close eye on your children; they may dart back inside to rescue a favourite toy.
*   Never re-enter the house until the fire brigade says it is safe to do so.

If you are cut off in an upstairs room by a fire:
*   Close the door to the room, close any fanlight above and use bedding, etc, to seal the gaps around the door.
*   Go to the window and shout for help.
*   If smoke gets into the room, lean out of the window. If smoke outside prevents this, lie on the floor until you hear the fire brigade arrive.
*   If conditions are so bad that you must attempt to escape before the fire brigade arrives, make a rope by knotting sheets together. Tie one end to the bed or a heavy item of furniture. If you have nothing with which to make a rope, drop cushions or bedding from the window to break your fall. Go through the window feet first, lower yourself to the full extent of your arms and drop. If your room is above the first floor, drop only as a last resort.
*   If the window will not open, break the glass with some-thing heavy like a chair. Try to clear as much of the glass as you can from the lower edge of the window frame and place a thick cloth over the sill before escaping.

FIRE DETECTION

Nearly a quarter of all domestic fires and half of all fire fatalities occur between 10 pm and 8 am. Obviously, during this period when most people are asleep a fire will very soon gain hold and burn undetected for a long time. By the time the occupants of the house wake up – if they wake up at all – it may be too late make good an escape. Similarly, a fire may break out in an unoccupied room during the day and burn undetected for some time, especially if only one or two people are in the house and occupying a room well removed from the one in which the fire is burning.

It is essential, therefore, that you have some means of detecting any fire as quickly as possible which will provide a warning in time for the occupants of the house to escape unharmed. This is most likely to be achieved with a smoke detector rather than a heat detector, and most fire detectors for domestic use are of the former type. They are usually self-contained battery-operated devices with their own loud sirens.

For maximum protection, a smoke detector should be fitted in every room including the loft but not the kitchen where it may be triggered accidentally by steam, etc – a heat detector is better here. However, a useful compromise can be provided by siting one detector in the hall and another on the upstairs landing. These will 'test' the air in your main escape route and sound the alarm long before it becomes unusable through smoke. Most smoke detectors can be linked together so that if one detects smoke it will automatically trigger the alarms of the others connected to it. Very often, it is possible to wire them into the control unit of a burglar alarm system.

Installation of a smoke detector is very easy – you simply screw it to the ceiling or high up on a wall. Most units are quite compact and unobtrusive.

It is important that you buy a smoke detector that has a test facility so that you can check it is still working at regular intervals. The battery should be replaced every year and most units give an audible warning signal when the battery power is getting low in case you have forgotten to change it.

FIRE FIGHTING

Although any major outbreak of fire should be left for the fire brigade to deal with, small outbreaks can often be caught in time before they have a chance to do much damage and it is essential to have some means of containing and killing small fires. There are two weapons available to the householder: the fire blanket and the fire extinguisher; ideally examples of both should be kept in accessible positions in the most vulnerable areas of the house – the kitchen and the garage.

All fires need oxygen to burn and the purpose of the fire blanket is to stifle the fire by cutting off its oxygen supply. Most fire blankets are made from a fibreglass material but make sure you buy one that does not contain asbestos. They are usually kept in a wall-mounted container from which they can be pulled quickly when needed. In use, the blanket should be held in front of you like a shield and draped quickly over the fire which should be left for some time to go out; the blanket can be used time and time again. Fire blankets are ideal for coping with fat fires and also car engine fires so it is a good idea to keep one handy in the car as well.

Fire extinguishers come with various types of filling to cope with particular types of fire. When you buy an extinguisher make sure you get one that is easy to operate – many have a simple trigger – and preferably one that does not discharge all of its contents in one go but rather in short controllable bursts. Read the operating instructions and make sure the rest of your family does so, too. Then fit the extinguisher where it can be readily seen and reached easily – most come with simple spring clip wall brackets.

One important point to remember with fire fighting is that unless you are absolutely certain that you can deal with the situation without endangering others or yourself, leave it to the fire brigade. It may hurt to have to stand back and watch your house burn, but this is nothing compared to the anguish and sorrow you or your family would suffer should someone perish in the fire in an attempt to fight it.

INFORMATION SOURCES

British Insurance Association
Aldermary House
Queen Street
London EC4N 1TU

British Standards Institute
Park Street
London

Fire Protection Association
Aldermary House
Queen Street
London EC4N 1TU

Health and Safety Executive Information Bureau
Chepstow Place
London

Home Security Magazine
Argosy House
High Street
Orpington
Kent BR6 OLW

National Supervisory Council for Intruder Alarms
St. Ives House
St. Ives Road
Maidenhead
Berkshire SL6 1RD

Royal Society for the Prevention of Accidents
Cannon House
The Priory Queensway
Birmingham

INDEX

accidents in the home 82
alarm sensors 57–61
alarm sounders 62
alarm systems 14, 56–77
  central stations 67, 76
  control units 63–64
  installation 69–71

bicycles 29
bolts 7, 12, 13, 14, 15, 17, 21
  window 18

callers (identifying) 17, 49–55
cars 9
cash boxes 31, 32, 40
closed-circuit TV 49, 52–54
Crime Prevention Officer 7
cylinder latches 11–12, 13, 21

door chain 7, 17, 49
door frames 6, 7, 11
door limiter 7, 17, 49
door locks 7, 11–17
doors 8, 11, 14, 17, 56

entry 'phones 51

false alarms 71–74
fire detection 93
fire fighting 94
fire risk 86–91

ground-floor extension 6

hiding places (for
  valuables) 31
holiday times 9

identifying marks 24
identification records 30
insurance 26, 31–32, 78–81

keys 8, 9, 13, 14, 17
  duplication of 14
  hiding 8
  skeleton 13

ladders 6, 9, 83
lights 10, 41–48
  automatic control of 42–43,
  46
  outdoor 44–48

lock picks 13
locking up 8–9, 18
locks 7, 11–23
locksmith 15

marking methods 26–30
milk delivery 9
mortice locks 13, 14, 15
movement detection 64, 76
multi-plane locks 14
multi-point locks 14

neighbourhood watch schemes
  10
newspaper delivery 9, 10

occupied look (of house) 9
outbuildings 7, 23

padlocks 14, 23
panic button 61, 74, 76–77
patio doors 6–7, 21
personal attack alarms 75
postal deliveries 9, 10

remote signalling devices 62, 77

safes 31–40
security marker pen 28
stay and catch 6
surface-mounted locks 14, 15,
  21, 22

viewing systems 7, 43–51

window frames 6, 11, 17, 18
  metal 17, 20–21
  wooden 17, 18, 21, 22
window locks 6, 17
  buying 21–22
  fitting 123
window panes 6
windows 6, 8, 56
  bathroom 6
  French 6–7, 21
  ground floor 6
  patio 6–7
  roof 6
  sash 20
  transom 6, 8
  upstairs 6, 8